THE LONG ARC
OF HOPE

THE LONG ARC OF HOPE

JAMES CLARKE

singular fiction, poetry, nonfiction, translation, drama, and graphic books

Library and Archives Canada Cataloguing in Publication

Title: The long arc of hope / James Clarke.
Names: Clarke, James, author.
Description: Poems. | Includes index.
Identifiers: Canadiana (print) 20220214735 | Canadiana (ebook) 20220214743 |
  ISBN 9781550969733 (softcover) | ISBN 9781550969740 (EPUB) |
  ISBN 9781550969757 (Kindle) | ISBN 9781550969764 (PDF)
Classification: LCC PS8555.L37486 L66 2022 | DDC C811/.6—dc23

Published by Exile Editions
144483 Southgate Road 14, Holstein, Ontario, N0G 2A0
www.ExileEditions.com
Printed and bound in Canada by Imprimerie Gauvin

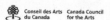 

We gratefully acknowledge the Canada Council for the Arts,
the Government of Canada, the Ontario Arts Council, and
Ontario Creates for their support toward our publishing activities.

Canadian sales representation: The Canadian Manda Group,
664 Annette Street, Toronto ON M6S 2C8.
www.mandagroup.com 416 516 0911

North American and international distribution, and U.S. sales:
Independent Publishers Group, 814 North Franklin Street,
Chicago IL 60610 www.ipgbook.com toll free: 1 800 888 4741

In memory of
Vince Wall

PROLOGUE

Accept the Blessing

In this desperate time of empty days
      and shapeless nights—locked in
separate cells where isolation and
      the distance between us force
everyone to drift down
      long unlit corridors, unanchored
and untouched—and you can
      feel life sliding away from you…

these poems are for you, friend:
      to free you to believe again in
the power of the breathing word
      to bind and heal old wounds and fears…
to remind you of the lushness of life's
      soft flesh and all the small missing
blessings that make life worth living,
      how deeply we belong and need one
another, and that love shapes all.

A PANDEMIC JOURNEY

*Only when we are brave enough to
explore the darkness will we discover
the infinite power of our own light.*
—BRENÉ BROWN

At a Crossroads

The winter solstice is upon us, days grow
darker. Humankind has been slowly
tearing our planet asunder. Now we're
distancing ourselves from each other in
wider and wider orbits, the future hurtling
toward us like a terrible nemesis.

Are we speeding through darkness to
some kind of light, or a new deadlier
pandemic? Will the kidnapped
Babe ever be restored to his manger, our
children feel safe again in their homes?
Can hope be reborn? Is it too late to heal
the wounds of Mother Earth?

Advent means arrival. We've arrived at a
crossroads. How much time do we have,
O God? When will we learn to see the world
with the gaze of love?

Where Now, Lord?

Where are we going, Lord? In the pandemic
we lurch forward—a fearful growing exodus
that seems to have no end. Everyone moves
in scraggly formation, the young pushing
from behind, the old exhorting us to
keep in line, and there's no turning back.

What Red Sea will we have to ford, Lord?
What salvific vaccine awaits us? We need Your
help, Lord, to overcome our over-the-cliff
foreboding that the life we have known will
be forever changed, to believe that we are
safe, that this too shall pass.

A Feather Without a Wing

Lately, sealed in the solitude
            of the pandemic, I feel
like the helpless blue-needled
            dragonfly with broken
wing I found floundering
            in the water by my
dock, or sometimes even
            like an arm without
a hand, unable
            to reach out, hug and
hold those dearest to me. I
            long for all the missing links—
"the old taken for granteds"
            that once gave normal
life its colour and meaning—
            like the blank, blue page

of opening morning sky that
            used to beckon me to fly and
write my dreams and hopes on,
            but doesn't any more.
            (inspired by Matt Moreland)

Future Shock

Something is happening. Citizens no longer freewheel
down beltways, lizards are panting at the springs,

tractors rust in fields. A virus sweeps across the land,
the violet hour closes up and eyes turn inward. Life

as we know it is changing; we're losing touch with
family and friends. Those old rose-tinted freedoms we

enjoyed with others are no longer welcome; nobody
suffers the peril of the warm embrace as an ankle twists

from the body being pushed away. We live in dread
of bruising those we love the most, then don't know

what to think or do. As night descends, we light
a candle, hunker down behind closed doors

to await the dawn—our little flame aflicker between
two great darks, fearful of who we will become and

what will happen next.

Crazy Thoughts

He remembered times as a judge,
        engulfed by the clamorous rhetoric
of lawyers all day, leaving the
        courtroom at night heart clogged
with the toxins of acrimony and
        wounded spirits, being so crushed
by the weight of a deeply flawed
        humanity he couldn't imagine any fate
worse,

until this bloated darkness of pandemic
        arrived with its small cruel robberies of
the mind and a relentless undertow of
        an alien silence—no more visits
with friends or Sunday family gatherings, the
        windows of heaven seemingly closed
and no escape but to draw the quiet
        sheets around you like a shield, yield
to the fleeting seduction of dreams.

A Senior's Prayer

Decrepitude besieges me, Lord. My eyesight's failing.
Under the humming grids of fluorescent lights I can

no longer read the 'best before' dates. Today, downtown,
I spied a homeless man dragging a wheelchair behind

him with a rope. I began to question why You allow our
relentless memories to load us down like donkeys

with the painful freight of old regrets, as though the
routine miseries of life itself were not punishment

enough. Now with sunlight leaving, the mind darkening
in these isolating times of Covid-19, I have resorted

to self-help, installed thick curtains on all the windows
to block out the threatening world outside, but fear

and old age keep thundering in. Some days I feel so
low I'm unsure I can continue. Have mercy on Your

children, Lord, who belong to the frail fellowship of the
stricken; wean us from our self-pitying ways, grant

us courage to trust and persevere.

The Dethroning of Death

Covid time has not been kind
        to the old consolation of the "good death"
surrounded by ritual, family and friends.
        Death was once a powerful god and
people built ships of death
        laden with beloved treasures to comfort
the deceased on their sacred passage
        into the great unknown.

Today with death dethroned,
        the dying—badgered by nurses, stupefied
by drugs and enmeshed in a
        bewildering web of life-support systems—
too often die as victims, lonely and unsung,
        accompanied only by strangers...death
just another fearful and nasty secret.

Kindness Lights the Way

Sometimes when overwhelmed by
the world's pandemic, and we feel
disheartened and isolated, banned
from friends, loved ones and the
consolation of sacred places—God
hidden under a blanket of silent,
sombre clouds with only a glimmer
of light to point the way—we are
tempted to give up and retreat
into some deep cave where no one
can ever reach us.

But when we notice someone at
the market go out of their way to help
a stranger in need, or read of caregivers
risking their lives at the bedsides
of the sick and dying, the curtain
of darkness will sometimes part, and
light pours in like an unstoppable
gift to raise our spirits, reminds us
that we're not orphaned, that our
shadowy path is strewn with hints
of loving kindness, and hope is reborn
anew.

Hope in a Time of Pandemic

Take pity on us, Lord, Your frail lost
            children, who can no longer taste
the honey of Your words,

sleepwalk with half-closed eyes in
            a state of amnesia, long sour faces
full of self-pity, our hope

like water where
            a watershed divides, falling
away from itself, feeling

we are on the brink of tumbling
            into a vast dark sinkhole with no one
there to notice or care, forgetful

of the great secret You wove into
            our hearts before we were born:
that mercy is the warp and woof

of the universe, and You are
            wholly with us in our weakness,
waiting to catch us when we fall.

Liberation Prayer

I'm weary of waking in this
                pandemic prison every morning
feeling desiccated, disconnected and
                discouraged, cut off from friends
and family, my vacant days and empty
                nights disappearing like the dew.

I ask Your help, Lord, to coax my
                closeted heart out of hiding, give me
the grace to see Your world with the
                eager eyes of a child, glimpse again
the stars beyond the stone-grey clouds.
                Only the fire of Your spirit can burn
away my fears and anxieties,
                free me from this steel-cold cell.

Pilgrimage of Light

In this time of pandemic—
                lost in a dark woods without the
old markers of day and night to
                keep my passage sure—as I begin
to lose hope of finding a clear
                path through the darkness,
a small voice deep within me
                whispers: *Don't despair, rest on the*
solid ground of here and now,
                the way beneath your feet neither
coming nor going, and
                let silence come alive in your
soul, shedding a healing light
                different from any source you've
ever known, revealing who
                you are and nothing less.

You are on a pilgrimage of light.
                Like Time, stand still in the dark; the light
knows where you are, let it find you.

The Quiet Conspiracy of Goodness

Praise to you, Lord, in this time of pandemic,
>for the sweet-scented air so full of brilliant
light, the ethereal pale-green burgeoning of fresh
>leaves and the colourful splash of new spring
flowers. We are beset by dark waves of
>doubt, death and uncertainty, Lord, need
the light and beauty of Your creation.

Praise to you, Lord, for all Your people
>of the heart around the globe of every
race, colour and creed, who go about
>the small labours of love each day unsung—
the person who volunteers on a refugee committee
>or picks up cast-off garbage in parks, aids
a disabled senior to cross a street, or the countless
>caregivers who daily risk their lives caring for
victims of the virus—all those who,
>by their way of seeing and being on the earth,
build a gentler, more hopeful world.

Praise to you too, Lord, for our kinship with this
            invisible company of brothers and sisters—
the only church where I long to be—
            whose quiet conspiracy of goodness gives
us wings to rise above the turbulent sea of hard
            times, helps redeem the world from chaos.

Spring Reverie

Now that April is opening its quiet eyelids to
the burgeoning beauty of the world again,

my heart longs to quit the locked, beleaguered
city, go back to Limerick Lake as trilliums lift

their small fragile voices above the quickening
earth in praise, and where the abandoned

farmhouse with the rusty clasp on its old storm door
sits along the winding cottage road, stop to feel

the choking weight of Covid's dark winter drop
away, contemplate the slanting morning sunlight

as it catches the cloudy heads of wild lilacs and
linger there among them, the air so inscrutably

free and fresh, just breathing in the blessing.

Hope for Tomorrow

The virus descended, stealthy and unseen,
like a thief in the night, squeezed its dark
glove around our hearts. Now, inside senior
care homes cruel thefts of mind and
body mount: medics in intensive care units,
frazzled and exhausted, race to save lives;
researchers in labs work round-the-clock
for a vaccine against the nemesis of time.

But just when all seems hopeless, and we
begin to doubt if spring will ever come,
the single, sharp cry of a crow—like a clean
knife—pierces the grey fabric of our lives
and it is enough, just enough, to lighten the
dark turning of our days, let us hope again.

FROM THE HEART
OF THE POET-JUDGE

To hear courteously, to answer wisely,
to consider soberly, and to decide impartially.
—SOCRATES

The Old Poet-Judge

was in the habit of wandering through
woods, listening to the whisperings of
trees, discovering hidden thoughts and
feelings in the rustle of leaves. At night,
the bluster and chaff of the courtroom
forgotten, he'd often stand star-struck
before the unending fields of heaven
thinking he could hear God's breath
behind His veil of silence.

Sometimes, in the stillness of a winter's
night, he'd hear the echo of God's voice
sifting down in gently falling snow. Only
when the unbreathable in him became
breathable were his poems able to speak
heart-to-heart to others.

Carnival of Law

Your stroll will take you through
a midway of odd sounds and sights:
lawyers doing verbal cartwheels to
catch a judge's ear, jurors locked
in a mock jury room searching for
a key, victim stranded high on a
stalled Ferris wheel demanding to be
rescued, and on a large dais a judge,
throat parched dry as straw,
breathing balls of fire.

And if you're still curious and brave
enough to journey on, the calliope will
pipe louder till at last you come to the
House of Mirrors crammed with people
just like you, and be shocked to see
your own distorted face.

The Long Wait

Consider this: during daylight hours
the judge rides the tiger of right and
wrong, looking for guilt or innocence, knows
the Temple of Law, flawed by human
frailty, rests on shifting foundations.
Evenings, after he dismounts and goes
home, frustrated by his inability to
reshape the world and its warped ways,

he retreats into his garden. As he
watches the last red-stained rays of light
dying on the horizon, he contemplates in
silence his defeats, the things he would
but cannot change, but still nurses the
hope of divine light, wondering how long
he'll have to wait.

Prelude

After a restless night's sleep, the judge was
driving to court to decide who would get

custody of the five-year-old daughter in a vexing
matrimonial case when he got stalled in a blinding

snowstorm. He began to spin his tires on the
icy asphalt and, as the snow grew thicker and

vehicles lined up behind him, he could only move
in fits and starts. He began to fear he wouldn't

make it to the courthouse that day. Wedged in
indecision, trapped on all sides by the snowy

ambivalence of fields, he started to vacillate,
wondering what he'd do, baffled how he'd

ever find a clear path through all the whiteness.

Painting the Law

Blend your colours well, grey's the colour of choice.

In the adversarial world of "he said, she said," the
overlapping folds of truth invariably blur.

To achieve the desired uniform tone, smooth the
paint with a wide brush—a palette knife will do—
to get a smoky hue.

Be lavish with your paint, eliminate any glints or
tints of bright pigment.

Afterwards, step back and contemplate your creation;
leave nothing to chance, find a suitable neutral
frame.

You'll know it's finished and ready for viewing when
no one can agree on what it meant to say.

Entitle it: *Many Shades of Grey*

The Judge's Three Tasks

First, slash through
falsehoods and fabrications,
uncover the unvarnished facts.

Keep an eye for biases.

Second, see each offender
as the person they are—
a person whose entire life
shaped their behaviour.

In this regard you will need
a determined mind and
will often falter.

Third, never let relevant legal
principles obscure the particulars of the
case that drive you to find a just
and compassionate resolution.

Regarding this one, call me when
your prayers are answered.

(inspired by David Budbill)

Wrong Forum

In the furnace of law where
      the aggrieved come for vindication,
to unfold their long spreadsheets
      of victimhood, seeking a permanent
fix for their troubled lives,

there are no exits or vistas of
      hope along the long, narrow
corridors to the fresh open air,
      nor alleluias of deliverance or
tambourines of thanksgiving...

only the jarring beat of the
      drums of counsel and the stern-cold
voice of justice can be heard—
      an echo chamber of fiery words.

Tarnished Halo

His appointment to the Bench
was hailed a victory. A man of
the people, everyone agreed,
endowed with the common
touch. At his swearing-in he
spoke humbly, said he felt like
he'd died and gone to heaven.

Now, you rarely see him any
more. Who could have foretold
the transformation, how the
pomp of his elevation took root
in his soul, created a little god
with a dismissive tongue, his
halo tarnished.

Roadkill

Driving home after

        a disturbing day in court

presiding over a bitter

        custody battle involving

an only child,

        the old judge glimpsed

too late the squirrel

        on the road…saw it stop,

hesitate, then change its

        mind…elected to keep his

undeviating line, shocked to glance

        back in his rear-view mirror to

see a clump of crimsoned fur

        crushed flat, black tail

fluttering on the asphalt, but

        even more appalled at how

callously the tyranny

        of choice can toss litigants into

the sharp claws of the law.

Custody Battle

Tomorrow is judgment day. The judge
retires early but can't sleep. His mind
is fogged in indecision. At midnight he

goes back to his study and hunches over
the thick file, glances at a photo of the
beautiful seven-year-old girl. Chin in

hand, he reviews the evidence and notes
his jottings in his bench book—*an unhappy
marriage…tawdry conduct on*

*both sides…the parties aggressive and
vindictive…feel pity for the child*. Outside,
black clouds press down, no starlight

to help him avoid the sharp edges
of the law. All these words and still no
light. With the hours ticking away and

unable to find a clear path through the `
welter of *he saids, she saids* the judge
finally goes back to bed, lies awake

waiting for the first light of dawn to
break, wondering into whose fangs he'll
toss the young girl's tender flesh.

The Rape

She remembered prickly grass under
          her yellow cotton dress, the sharp

ridges of the uneven ground, his thick
          wrists, blunt fingers around her

throat and his sour breath on her
          face, the iron muscle between her

legs…but mostly it was the mantra
          she remembered, *you bitch, you*

bitch, you bitch—the voice detached
          as though talking to someone else, a

mother, a wife, a stranger—but no matter
          how hard she tried she could never

remember his head. *Styrofoam*, she finally said,
          the kind you see in a store window;

he could be anyone.

Shaken Baby Syndrome

The stricken parents, both young
                professionals, did everything by the
book—vetted several agencies,
                interviewed candidates, even visiting
their homes to select the perfect
                caregiver for their firstborn child.
Before finding the woman guilty
                of causing death the new judge,
knowing how important it was
                for the parents' closure to learn what
occurred, clinically and systematically
                reviewed all the evidence and relevant
law, carefully skirting the one mystery
                why, which he didn't know how to
answer—a question that, long after
                he applied the gauze of law, continued
to hover over his conscience like a black,
                impenetrable cloud.

Holy Thursday

In the Egypt of Landlord and Tenant court
at Brampton this Holy Thursday,
where a throng from
all races, creeds, and walks of life
murmurs in the rotunda:
tenants who can't pay rent,
landlords who can't pay mortgages,
unemployed fathers,
single welfare moms,
the mentally afflicted,
the physically disabled,
scoundrels, saints, everyone

lugging a sack of bad luck—
no money, no job, Powers of Sale, leaky
roofs, faulty furnaces, flooded basements,
dripping faucets, attic squirrels,
sudden sickness, government treachery,
hungry children,
runaway husbands (etc.)—

there are no tambourines
of thanksgiving,
just the rough deliverance
of the law,
with no paschal blood
on the doorposts
to guide my slippery sword.

Rush to Judgment

The Hell's Angel with
locks the colour of dandelions,
pink muscle T-shirt and gold earrings—a blue
skeleton on a motorcycle, RIDE HARD,
DIE FREE tattooed on his right
bicep—shambled to the witness
box and testified
how he saw the blue Cutlass skid
into the concrete
abutment, stopped his bike and
stayed with the woman whose legs were jammed
under the steering column,
stroking her
hand, whispering to her like a lover, and
lost his job as bouncer
at the Brass Rail all-day
strip club for being late.

Sometimes I Feel Pity

for the not-so-good thief,
you know, the one who leaves finely sculpted
footprints in snowdrifts and perfect fingerprints
on fridge doors, florid calling cards;
the hapless creature
who, nabbed red-handed with the smoldering goods
in the back of the open pick-up,
is struck speechless until
at the station
he opens his heart to the first officer
who promises to be his friend,
sealing the alliance
with a signed inculpatory statement.
Yes, there has to be a place
in paradise even for the clumsy thief,
whose simplicity
makes us want to, like
Jesus, forgive
his artless mischief.

The Long Reach of Guilt

The testimony of the young man—how
he flew into a rage when a miniature
Doberman peed on his new car, smashed
a tire iron so violently on the dog's head
it died—

brought back a long-buried memory of
the judge's father, after he'd come home
from the war and caught him shooting
grackles in the neighbour's maple with a
BB gun, pretending they were German
Stukas crashing through the rustling leaves…
the fury of his father's thunderous voice
as he axed the BB gun to smithereens:
I'll do ya, lad, if I ever catch you killing
birds again,

his whole body beginning to shake under his
black silk robes as though it was 1946 and all
happening again.

Child Molester

He was not a harsh judge,

gave the accused a speedy trial,

the benefit of reasonable doubt, and then

a just verdict and the gold milk of mercy.

Everything within his power he gave, save

the one thing he needed most:

he couldn't find a sentence that included forgiveness.

Nor could the inmates, of

the grey prison underworld where they sent him,

who slit his throat.

Majestic Chords

In court today—an acrimonious matrimonial dispute—
the evidence disclosed that the mother and father, poised

on either side of their dying son's hospital bed, had
engaged in a fierce tug-of-war over his medical chart,

and finally had to be separated by the nursing staff. The
judge went home early that day—feeling frustrated and

speechless, the snarl of the couple's voices still echoing
in his ears—sought solace in the sunroom. Uplifted by the

majestic chords of Bach's *Magnificat* on the radio,
he watched grey and black squirrels in the garden scurrying

along the fences and branches of the maples, gnashing,
clawing and snapping at each other, enacting with

blithe indifference—their own rendition of an unforgiving
and pitiless world.

Prison Art Therapy

The murderer portrayed the prosecutor as a
black-robed executioner swinging a sword with

both fists and a stricken neck flowering into a
hundred rosettes. Another inmate, a notorious

thief, sketched a stick figure caught by a spider
with eight wire-thin legs in the centre of her orb.

Near the door, the bank robber painted a Robin
Hood with fiery eyes, face streaked with green

rashes, taking aim with a bow and arrow. The
rapist from the west coast drew a woman's face,

blank save for one giant furious eye. The old lifer,
whose job it was to water the prison plants and

weed the flowers, dashed off a charcoal portrait of the
angel Lucifer wearing a benign smile and a jaunty

straw hat. *It's taken a long time*, he said, *but
I've finally made my peace with the devil.*

Winter Reprieve

After a frustrating day
 in the steamy laundry
of the law—lawyers
 gnashing it out like
warrior gods, words
 flying off their tongues
like blackbirds
 leaving snowy spaces—
the old judge,
 hoping to forget
for a moment the legal
 blizzard raging inside
the courtroom,
 withdrew to the
sanctuary of his
 chambers, was rattled to
see, sitting in his parking space
 outside his window,
a stray black mongrel,
 staring defiantly up at him
as though the spot
 was legally his.

Looking at this glacial
         world, the judge knows
there is no sorcery to
         free him from the cold
clutches of the law.

What the Judge Failed to Mention

In sentencing the young man to prison the
judge told him, *I hope you have learned that*

crime does not pay. What the judge failed
to mention were all the other lessons the

young man would learn in that underworld
of stone, where everyone is allotted a small

wedge of unreachable sky and redemption's
in short supply, where love belongs to a lost

language and everyone drinks from the same
wormwood cup, where you wake each dawn

in a sunless cell too small to dream, left to
wonder where the light of the world has fled.

Reprieve

Dispirited by the rancorous
      behaviour of litigants in
his courtroom,
      the old judge sat on
his deck with his
      morning coffee, uncertain
how much more he
      could endure of their antics,
when a damselfly with
      sapphire wings, glints of
sunlight aslant its abdomen,
      alighted on his shoe, reminding
him once more how
      quickly the beauty of creation
could restore his spirit,
      make him momentarily forget
the follies of
      a flawed humanity.

Daydreamer

Beleaguered by a
          thicket of bewildering
laws, and hollowed out
          by the verbal juggleries
of lawyers, the judge
          often felt stymied
and trapped in a net
          of words—unable to
escape or decide.

One morning, observing
          a mite skittering
across a blank page
          of his bench book,
he let his imagination drift,
          encircled it in thick
red ink hoping
          the mite would
discover an exit through
          the sticky red barrier
and show him
          a way out of
his own predicament.

That's when an irate lawyer,
          thinking he was nodding
off, dropped a Bible on the floor
          with a loud bang, startling
him back to the real world.

Equality in the Law

This blustery January morning,
              just as the judge finished
sermonizing in court on his
              favourite hobby horse—
inequality in the law—
              the fire alarm ripped through
the courtroom, expelling everyone
              outside to face the lash of winter.

The judge suddenly found himself,
              in robe and red sash, on
the icy steps of the
              courthouse, huddled and
shivering with a motley
              crowd of jurors, accused,
litigants, police, attendants—everyone
              waiting for the all-clear
bell to sound—the hierarchy
              of the court suspended by
the white equality of snow.

An Awkward Moment

When the judge, who was known for his
          observance of the deferential niceties of
the court, entered the courtroom that
          day, he noticed that the white-haired
lawyer at the counsel table didn't rise as
          was the protocol. Glowering, he remarked,
It's the practice in this court for counsel
          to stand when a judge enters the courtroom.

But after the words had escaped his tongue
          and he observed the lawyer struggle to his
feet, heard him groan as he leaned sideways
          to pick up his cane off the floor and say,
I apologize, Your Honour, he wished
          with all his heart that he could have hidden
himself in the dark holding cells below.

Valedictory of a Jaded Judge

Old age lays no golden thoughts so don't
      be shocked if I set you straight. The court's
no place to pick a fight, your hope of closure
      is far from bright. Though Law and Mercy
share the same border and need to cooperate,
      Law's a bully who likes to cross over. In
brief, trusting the law can be a big mistake.

But consider the alternative: no judges,
      no lawyers, no courthouses, no laws—
just ordinary folk like you and me, eyeball
      to eyeball, barbed hearts intact, bashing
it out with stones and clubs. Either way
      the result's the same: a tsunami of grief.

When the Jaded Old Judge

cramped between regrets
          of the past and
fears of the future,
          begins to shove off
the dead weight
          of the law, gives
up his fruitless quest
          for perfect justice
in a flawed world, and
          accepts what he
can neither change
          nor understand,

he may yet learn
          to reopen his heart,
yield to the language
          of the senses, see
the lush beauty of creation
          with the fresh expectant
eyes of a child,
          greet the spring
rains with the
          unconditional YES
of open hands.

Apocalyptic Dream

Three years before the old judge's retirement, the dreams
started. So many lawyers bickering among themselves

like warrior gods, words flying off the page like drones
creating desolate spaces, old law books suddenly

indecipherable. Judges gathered at the coffee bar to
clear their heads, worry, worry, everyone at a loss

wondering if the world was falling apart. In the blinding
white-out the old judge stopped writing judgments.

What was the use? Nothing seemed to make sense any
longer; all he could think to do was hunker down in

an alcove of the courthouse, imagine a tall tale of three
arctic explorers lost in an amnesia of snow, and say

to himself this story won't have a happy ending.

Moments of Doubt

There are days when the judge leaves
    the courthouse after a frustrating,
unsuccessful day trying to bridge the
    differences between embattled and
intransigent litigants,

goes home to watch the news unfurl,
    the recycling of the earth's grim
stories—abuse of corporate power, rape of
    Mother Earth, treachery of governments,
all the jagged debris of a broken world—

tumbles into bed late at night, feeling
    powerless as a child before a deeply
flawed humanity, half convinced that all his
    good intentions are just airy fantasies...
only to rise like the sun next morning,

hope in his heart mysteriously
    restored, resolved to try once more.

One Remaining Consolation

After years in the labyrinth
            of law coping with our flawed
humanity—the insurgencies of
            the divided heart—trying to find
in the arena of the courtroom
            the secret alchemy that transmutes
the strident rumblings of antagonism
            into the quiet voice of reason
(even berating himself at times for
            accepting the invidious role
of judging others) the old judge
            finally gave up his dream of perfect
justice, would shed his heavy robes
            together with all his good intentions,
return home evenings, his mind
            at peace, content that he had done
his best, his one remaining consolation:
            a good night's rest.

The Pragmatist

After decades plucking nettles and thorns from
the law, deciding what should stay, what should
go—a vexing, never-ending task—the old judge, who'd
only recently turned eighty-seven, began to ask
himself if he'd ever accomplished anything that lasts.
What am I looking for now? Is it love? A good night's
rest? Or death?

As a pragmatist, like most of his colleagues on the
bench—keepers of the holy order of things who
try to explain the changing rules that keep us safe
for human habitation, but never the ones that
confound us most, what to live for—he brushed aside
these questions to face his last great hurdle: learning
to live with the imperfections that still cluttered the
weedy garden of his own life.

A Judge's Dreamwish

If I were empowered
to begin afresh and reconstruct the law,
going to court would

mark a new beginning:
no more bluff and bluster, no more barbed
words volleying back and

forth; instead, I'd open
a sitting to celebrate peace-making,
with special awards for

reconciliation and forgiveness,
rejoice as former foes dropped the rhetoric
of war, learned

the lost art of listening, how
to bite their tongues. Rather than a
pompous speech I'd propose a toast

of champagne to contrite
lawyers as they lined up to peacefully turn
in their verbal knives and guns.

How sad to know
my dream is wishful thinking, but O
how I wish it were so.

The Last Wish List

After the reading the young poet approached the
judge with a question: *Why did you become a poet?*
The judge, who had taken up poetry after his wife's
death, had routinely answered that question many
times before but, on this occasion, his words
crumbled in his mouth.

The young poet would have unaccounted years
ahead to test the slopes of love, write her poems,
compile her own list of squandered affections, taste
the wormwood of failed dreams. When the judge
was young, he thought growing old a quaint illusion.
Now his unfinished wish list began to unscroll in his
head—keep evil at bay, disarm sharp tongues,
dampen the rancor and volatile passions that infect
the spirit, repair the world by applying the laws
fairly and with compassion, learn the lost dialect of
love, speak with the gentle voice of poetry and
reconciliation—till he drew back, realized his mind
had drifted into the deep, unchartable gulf between
his own past and the young poet's future, that he
hadn't answered her question.

The young poet, unfazed, had another question…
and still another.

What the Old Judge Learned

An old judge knows verbal scheming and
how words flow from the fertile minds
of legal advocates, and from his own pen.

When he reads the weave of a poet's words
...*riotous clouds, faltering earth, silvery earth,*
moonstruck night...a certain restlessness
settles in.

The judge and the poet come from different
worlds...or so we like to believe. Yet both
honour the gift of language, see in
and beyond words the mystic fire of silence.

A Water Jug

sits on my bench—
    a shiny vessel, clearer
than the eye of justice.
    Nine times each day,
my constable pours
    me a glass
to flush away
    the dark sediment
in my veins, keep
    the system pure.

Words, like aquifers,
    also nourish the
garden of law
    with life-giving waters
but, if used to subvert
    truth or obfuscate, they
turn toxic and
    justice withers,
no roots,
    no flowering.

Advice to a Newly Minted Judge

Judge with a compassionate heart,
    see the scars within the bruised souls
of those who appear before you. Turn
    your courtroom into a place of truth,
reconciliation and hope. Keep a listening
    heart, learn to hold your tongue.
Remember: a word of kindness reaches
    far, opens doors to grace and healing.

And when you find yourself in error,
    mean-spirited or smitten with self-
importance, retreat to your chambers,
    ask the icon of St. Francis on your desk
to infuse a note of gentleness into your
    legal world, halt your haughty ways.

GROWING UP
IN TOUGH TIMES

*Memories of childhood are the dreams
that stay with you after you wake.*
—JULIAN BARNES

Simcoe Street

No flowers grew on Simcoe Street;
crows circled round the house in pairs,
dandelions withered at our feet.

The brutal sun on sidewalk beat
and every dream was trampled bare,
no flowers grew on Simcoe Street.

Only the balm of frazzled sleep
provided armour you could wear,
dandelions withered at our feet.

Nor was there shelter we could seek
sodden nights when fists would flare;
no flowers grew on Simcoe Street.

Bruised bodies in a naked heap
were more than weeping eyes could bear;
dandelions withered at our feet.

Our days were one, long cold retreat
shivering down a wintry stair,
no flowers grew on Simcoe Street,
dandelions withered at our feet.

In My Town

we didn't say garden
but backyard.

We didn't say powder room
but toilet.

Not cocktails,
beer,

not full-figured,
fat.

We didn't eat fancy, but
macaroni, baked beans,
neck bones and leftovers.

We didn't get angry,
we fought and got even.

We had no money,
flowers, lawn, shade trees,
brand name clothes, vacations or
cars; there was no cure
for hopelessness…

tomorrow just another name for
disappointments and
broken dreams.

(inspired by Sally Fisher)

A Darker World

Shards of memory: wartime, a row
house in a rough neighbourhood of town,
headlines trumpeting the landings in
Normandy…my Dad's letters like scrawny
bluebirds exhausted from their long sea
voyage regularly tumbling through the
brass letter slot, clattering on the front
hall linoleum…a loving, protective mother
who lavished books on her firstborn only
son….

and then the time I rushed home with
a bloodied nose, told Mom the gang
across the tracks beat up my friend Abe,
called him a *kike* and *Jew-boy* and
I had tried to stop them. Before bed that
day when I asked her, *Why do people
hate Jews?* a pained expression flashed
in her eyes, followed by a long silence.
You did the right thing, son, she finally
said in a quiet voice. *I'm proud of you.*

That evening, unable to sleep, my mind
slowly opened to a different, darker
world.

First Love

I had a secret crush on Kitty
that year at school I had to repeat;
the pulley of my brain had gone crazy.

Her haughty British accent made all the
boys dizzy but, though too shy to compete,
I still kept my secret crush on Kitty.

Her long dark lashes made me giddy,
I left dozens of love poems incomplete;
the pulley of my brain had gone crazy.

People would've laughed and called me silly
had I confessed we didn't talk or meet;
no one could have guessed my crush on Kitty.

How often her sun burst on me brightly
and yet my bliss was never complete;
the pulley of my brain in action crazy.

O, how I now wish I'd dared more bravely
and planted a kiss on her coy, rosy cheek;
I had a secret crush on Kitty,
the pulley of my brain had driven me crazy.

Fathers and Sons

When he came home from Normandy, the
wounded hero, he carried deep inside him
a hidden rage. Gathering all his brokenness
and pain he built himself a box, stepped
inside, leaving me, his only son, to glimpse
him through slats of fading light. Separated
by a wall of silence, we rarely spoke,
never shared a meal together.

Nor did he ever talk about the war. Once
he caught me boasting in the backyard
to my friends about how he'd killed a
dozen Hitler Youth with a bayonet, rushed
out of the house, eyes ablaze and boxed
my ears. *If I ever catch ya talking like that
again, I'll do ya in, lad, I will,* he shouted.

Years later after his funeral I opened the
small box of his ashes, cast his wild Irish
dust into the gusting wind, but particles
of ash and bone kept blowing back. That's
when I realized I could never completely
free myself from his shadow, that we were
locked in the same box together. Forever.

Periwinkles

Every time I pass a fish market it is 1945, the year
Father came back from the war. He is hunched at
the kitchen table in the tenement on Simcoe Street

in khaki pants, blue flannel work shirt peeled back to
the elbows, a large galvanized pail on the oilcloth in
front of him. Father would never eat with the rest
of us, and after supper Mom would shoo us upstairs or
outdoors so he could be alone.

Years later I'd often wonder why he closed himself off,
never spoke about the war…but that is another story.
Periwinkles are my story, and the way Father would
bend at the table, a toothpick in thick awkward fingers,
and spear the slippery snails, the dark shells scattering
on the white linoleum like empty cartridges.

Adrift

Dusk…a dinghy floats in the middle
            of a lake, fog swirls across its
surface in ghostly pockets. A boy
            and his two sisters listen as
their mom and dad start to argue,
            rehashing old hurts and
grievances. Having heard it all
            before, the children shut
their eyes, cover their ears.

After a while tempers flare.
            Suddenly the man stands,
he can't take it anymore he
            shouts, leaps into the lake,
starts to swim towards shore.
            Furious, the woman quickly
dives in after him, tells
            the children not to worry,
she'll come back. As the voices
            and thrashing of water begin
to fade, the children panic,
            cry out, *Come back, come
back,* but their cries are

             answered by an eerie silence.
As night descends, the boy
             starts to row, the only sound
the soft thump of
             oarlocks in the dark.

Legacy

Nothing could stop you,
            not even the past...
that last spring when
            you knew you were
dying and planted
            red roses in the
weedy front yard—
            something you'd
never done before.

What new life were
            you trying to grow,
Father? You had
            no fondness for
flowers, or the small
            rites and adornments
of family living, slithered
            in and out of our lives
like a stranger.

When you slipped under
            the dark shadow of
death, before we got
            to know you or even
say goodbye, you left behind
            your only legacy: a dozen
withered red roses and
            short sharp-thorned
memories of you.

Absentee Father

Sometimes a father will return
               from the war and then
go away again in
               body, spirit and mind
so that he is not there
               for his son who never
gets to know him, and they
               remain strangers all
their lives. But the father
               won't let the son go,
haunts him nightly in dreams,
               keeps knocking on
the door of his heart
               to be let in.

Father, I was too young and
               slow to understand how
wounded you were.
               Now that you've joined
the wordless dead,
               it's too late for the countless
things we should have
               said but never will.
If you were still living,

and I knew where to find you,
I'd rap on your door.
Dear Father, I'd tell you,
I've waited too long to
know what I wanted
and needed to say:
I forgive you and love you.

The Lost Years

During the long stretch of
            childhood when time stood still
—years salted with tears, Dad
            overseas, Mom struggling to keep
us afloat—I'd escape the chronic
            worries of the house, hike to my
favourite haunt, Green Hill
            west of town…stop along the way
to play at the secluded marsh
            where bullfrogs with quiet bulging
eyes nudged along the edge…watch
            cars speeding past me on the dusty
road, the drivers staring straight
            ahead, wondering what secret
errands they were running.

Those were the lost years when
            I thought I was missing out on living,
wasting my time, always waiting
            for something to signal the beginning
of my real life in a wider world.
            Summer pulled a green sheet over
my head and I'd listen to the electric
            hum of roadside poles for portents
of a future that never seemed to come.

THE WAY OF THE ARTIST

*Poetry is boned with ideas, nerved and
blooded with emotions, all held together
by the delicate, tough skin of words.*
—PAUL ENGLE

The Way of the Artist

Not so much plotting
               what craft can do,
but how the river speaks in

its meander of green glass,
               a stepping back and
yielding to the moment's flow,

allowing the living river
               to shape its course,
a sharing and letting-go.

Ars Poetica

Those who only pay attention to the
syntax of things, insist on rigid
obedience to blind custom, miss the
slant beauty of things, never feel the
breathless anticipation of new realms
unfolding in the net of the heart.

Lovers listen for the soft shifting of
Eros, birds love to sing in variant keys.
Poets, like delicate glass wind chimes,
revel in the rainbow of refracted colour
and quiet music of sound, learn to let
their passion lead them where to go,
know that poetry is not a paragraph to
be parsed, but a wild song to be sung.

Be Prepared

I'm writing these poems for
you, reader, cracking open

my chest, letting you see the
rain inside my heart. Every

poem I make is a river
running through my fingers,

always altering shape. So
don't ask me to explain: like

a bowl of roses a poem
just is. But be prepared:

should you someday meet
a poem that speaks to you,

it could peel back old scars,
change your life in a way

you never dreamt of before.

Poet's Mission

To shake the tree
                of language
to its roots, one less
                word at a time, and
find under the
                flurry of fallen
words a few seeds
                of new life,

is to slowly clear
                a place of light,
where calm and stillness
                hold sway and
you can even hear
                dumb stones
buried in the earth begin
                to sing.

A Poet Speaks His Mind

Sometimes I see myself
                as a poetic dinosaur

because I like to write
                in rhyme. To see words

mate fills me with with
                sonic pleasure,

takes the measure
                of my skill as a poet,

and on occasion
                leads me to say things

that are, frankly, rude.
                Poets who disdain

rhyme are reticent
                prudes who, unlike turtle-

doves who love to
                cuddle and coo, recoil

in hasty distaste to see
                words making love.

Poetry-Making

is not a matter of
     standing outside in the cold
rain for long periods
     hoping to be struck by
lightning, or the trick
     of a sorcerer's like the
one famous for driving nails
     through glass
without leaving a mark, but

something more prosaic:
     plodding in solitude
in the same room
     at a same desk day in,
day out, trying to
     shape meaning out of
stiff-necked language,
     learning to braid frail
words into a rope
     strong enough to hang
your wet, well-worn
     clichés out to dry.

Word Haven

I envy the robin
            on maple bough
who leaf by leaf,
            twig by twig,
builds a sturdy
            brown nest—
a safe haven against
            the biting wind—

while I, a naked poet
            with neither twig
nor leaf, have only
            this small rampart
of frail words
            to blunt its
long sharp knives.

Winter Greening

I'm an old poet winnowed by loss,
     often shaken and burdened by the
morning news, the unending daily
     rages of the race, with only this
small cache of words to mend my
     brokenness…yet someone still thankful

to be alive, amazed at the misty
     radiance of the reborning sun,
clinging however waveringly to the
     invisible ladder of prayer, praising
every victory over meanness and
     indecency…each poem I write a frail
container of hope waiting to be
     opened at dawn.

Lost Voices

Swept along by
     our onrushing,
kaleidoscopic lives,
     there's no time
to swaddle the soul
     with poetry, read
as though the masters
     were still near
waiting in silence
     to make us pause
and reflect, set aglow
     our distracted minds
with radiant words…
     no time for the slow
turning of pages.

Poet's Lamentation

In the golden age the bards
                    gave birth to gods, then
fashioned out of mythic air
                    ambrosia—a delicious,
ethereal food—for them
                    to feast on.

How daunting today, Lord, for
                    Your poor wordsmiths
to feed the heart's famine.
                    Though we yearn to
channel the dazzling power
                    of Your awesome Being,
You always elude our porous
                    net of language.

Have pity, O Elusive, dimly
                    apprehended One, light our
tongues again, we pray,
                    with the mystic fire of words,
forgive our clumsy art.

Poetry on the Comeback

Swept away by the hurly-burly of
            our fast-paced lives, no one today has
time for the wonder of words.
            No one reads poetry anymore,
critics complain.

So I wasn't shocked when browsing
            in the Bookshelf Café I found that
poetry had disappeared from its
            usual place—the crucibles of silver
words abolished from the shelves,
            replaced by auto-therapy.
Sign of the times, I mused…

until, that is, the young woman
            at the desk led me down the aisle,
restored my faith in humanity,
            showed me shelves bulging with
poetry. *We've had to move
            poetry to a traffic area,* she said.
Thievery's on the rise again.

Flights of Imagination

The old poet afflicted
      with writer's block must
learn "to let go," turn
      his back on the stale dogmas
of convention and rhetoric,
      break the bonds of his earthly
chains—the gravity of empty
      words and deadened feelings—

invoke his muse to help
      him reinvent himself...imagine
he is a gull translucent
      against the sun, hollow bones
borne aloft on flights
      of imagination and wild thought,
an undercurrent of breathless
      wonder under his wings.

The Muse

Soon after he took up poetry, after his
         wife's suicide, the poet found that his
muse was an insomniac who'd stay up
         late at night, gazing at the motion of stars
or listening to the rustle of leaves, seeking
         answers to confounding questions like why
do bad things happen to good people,
         when all he wanted to do was sleep.

As time went on she became increasingly
         daring and independent. Despite his
misgivings, she began to make house calls
         to those places where the destitute dwell
and when he'd object *Why go there?*
         she'd admonish him for his hardness of
heart, remind him we are all called to help
         people get over the muddy ditches of
their lives (if we can). *Widen your heart,*
         poet, she'd say. *Remember, God reveals*
Himself in broken places.

The Sullen Muse

The poet needs
             the patient mind of
the carpenter to select the
             right words and nail images
together, plane the
             surface smooth and shiny.

Often when a fine powder
             rises to clog the tongue,
and words refuse to come,
             you'll see your sullen
muse—the one who
             left you in a huff—

standing outside your
             body, stiff and speechless…
begin to wonder if she'll ever
             pass her fingers through
the wind chimes
             of your poems again.

Cezanne's Wife

For decades,
      at his bidding
she modeled
      for him, endured
the blue fury
      of his intensity
without a murmur.

Observe the
      portraits, the
slow progression
      from slim figure, and
delicate oval face
      fresh as an apple,
to pale matron
      with heavy jowls—
the same look
      of stoic resignation.

Who, then or
      now, tracks the cost
of perfection,
      the quiet unsung acts
of self-giving love?

The Bearded Lady of Poetry

If you meet the Bearded
        Lady of Poetry in the schoolyard
don't shun or order her to leave;
        even worse, don't send her to the

principal for correction. The Bearded Lady is
        not computable; wants to be herself,
insists you accept her as she is.
        She desires not just your intellect but

your whole crystallized self—nerve
        endings, dreams, all five senses,
memory—everything that exists alive
        (though sometimes sleeping) in you that

you've forgotten how to say. She's a
        mystery to be revealed and, if you're
patient and curious, she may in her
        own good time tell you her secrets,

shape your understanding in ways
        beyond your imagination. She is a
wanderer; observe how she'll
        slip away outside the yard any

time, anywhere, and
          if you're ready she may even beckon
you to come along…let you follow
          her footprints into the snow-white light.

Elegy for the Written Word

In this art gallery of
            remaindered books,
dismembered, twisted and
            torn pages are braided
and sculpted into a novel
            collection of spreading tree
branches, filigreed
            butterfly wings, flying clouds
and other shiny baubles
            to dazzle the eye, icons
of a changing time—
            no patience for the
transformative word.

Walking the Corpse Home

The old poet, lost within himself, is "walking
home backwards" as they say in China. He has

assigned himself the hard work of memory,
refuses to die on some dusty road in a foreign

land far away from his hearth. Alert to the
hungry ghosts within him, he rises early to

track the morning sun, revisit old haunts and
hurts, determined to make amends for all the

defections and missteps of the first half of life,
when he was too callow and mindless to pay

attention. He is walking backwards to find
himself, living his life twice. He is going home.

THE INVITATION TO LOVE

*Being deeply loved by someone gives
you strength, while loving someone
deeply gives you courage.*
—LAO TZU

A Harsh and Fearful Thing

You created us, Lord,
        with a thirst for
permanence, showed us
        by Your sacrificial
cross the price of
        unconditional love.

We, Your creatures,
        know what it means
to be burdened with a
        dross-sack of dead dreams,
and pass through sunless days, to feel
        the pain of Your absence.

We long to believe, Lord,
        that You accompany
us on our journey,
        measure where we are
in time, sustain our
        every step with divine love.

We need help, Lord; it's a
        harsh and fearful thing
to love what death touches,
        especially when the beating
hearts of those we love grow still.

The Unspeakable Sadness of Angels

In the beginning there were only the two of them.
Those angels who preside over the dreaming human
spirit shuddered with delight on their cloudy perches
high above the stream as the woman draped herself
across the centre thwart, leaned back and grasped
the gunwales, while the man crept up from the stern
on hand and knee to begin the awkward ecstasy.

When the canoe tipped, tossing the couple into the
cold water, the angels at first chuckled. But as eons
yawned and fell back, and more and more earthlings
were swept away by the current, it slowly dawned on
their exotic minds that despite their unappeasable
longing for intimacy, no matter how closely the man
and woman embraced and rubbed against each
other, they could never become one creature, find the
still point that stays the lurch of gravity.

And when the angels observed the man and woman
begin to blame one another for their near-drownings
and disappointments, and realized that they would
never master the art of lovemaking in a canoe, that
this fault-finding would go on forever, an unspeakable
sadness overtook them and, folding their tinselly
wings, they hid their shining faces and wept.

The Road to Eden

Before you leave the lower frequency of love
you have to stumble hard. Once, I almost
slipped breathless beneath the icy waters of

grief, but then a hand reached down from
the burning crater of sky, touched my heart and
made me feel for the first time—don't ask

how or why—the tender gravity of love.
The road I was travelling on turned into
an earth-gold field, the evils I'd suffered

fell behind and I found myself in a quiet
place, blest, all the hard edges of my life
fastened together by the hasp of joy. I have

no idea what gate I'll step through next, but
I've begun. The love feast is not far off.

A Not So Solemn Promise

Every morning, fair weather, foul weather,
              a man sets out for the point across the
sheltered bay, a red, blue, white beach ball tied
              to his left ankle...his boy, wearing yellow
flippers swimming close behind—their summer ritual.
              Today they reach the point, clamber up its
steep slope to the granite ledge and gaze at the clouds
              streaming above the big windy lake, the
whitecaps racing in, the horizon almost invisible in
              morning mist. *One day, I'm gonna swim
all by myself to the other side,* the boy says, voice
              ringing with confidence. After a long pause
and without averting his eyes from the distant horizon,
              the man replies, *Yes, son, perhaps one day
you will.*

The Blessing
(for Mira and Greg)

Sometimes a longing unfolds
                into a hidden miracle
that honours the soul with
                an awesome gift.
Sometimes a man and
                a woman will weave
together a tapestry of love
                that becomes a blessing,
changes a "getting older"
                into a "getting younger,"
hear within the deep folds
                of their flesh the small
voice of a new creation
                asking to take its sacred
place as a guest of
                the universe, beloved
of the earth, that
                gladdens their hearts,
makes them clap and
                sing a new song
of gratitude and joy.

A Bouquet of Roses

The man who steps out
    of the flower shop into

the gathering dusk, a
    bouquet of roses clutched
in his awkward hands,
    is someone who has
travelled far, knows
    the cues he missed when
cornered or afraid,
    what it's like to wear
a blindfold round his
    heart, the *I love you's*—
that starved like beggars
    on his tongue when
someone was alive—that
    always came too late.

Though chastened by his
    blindness, he is not lost.
He's a man on a mission,
    thinking of someone dear,
determined to make amends,

    raise tenderness from its
squalor of neglect, swim
      against the past's cold
current. His roses shine
    in the dark.

Old Habits

Today, let us forget our worries and enjoy our favoured
breakfast—yogurt and berries. After, we'll resume our
daily habit, walk together the long corridors of the mall
before shops open with all the other retirees trying to
slow down the erosion of time, recoup the remnants of
their last years.

I'll tell you my latest dreams, grouse again about all
the pain my arthritis is causing lately. I might even
mention how winded I now get trying to tie my laces.
I'll be happy to hear you talk again about the boon of
staying fit, the swerves and shifts of our children's lives,
how you plan to fill your day. We'll dip into our
storehouse of old memories, reminisce about lost loved
ones and friends, perhaps even laugh or cry a little.

In listening to each other, we'll know we're the same
people we've always been—innocents of betrayal, intent
on affirming what remains of our changed lives. Yet,
despite slippages of memory, old hurts and disappointments,
we'll still pause to count our blessings. We know what this
day will bring, but we also know it deserves to be lived with
all the possibilities of the empty page.

Back home in our familiar setting, our old rhythm of
life will unfold seamlessly till bedtime when we'll
know the time's come to kiss and wish sweet dreams,
turn off the lights and wait the coming of night.

Where Are We Going?

They travelled together, as far north
            as the wetlands of Hudson's Bay, and
now they were wheeling south again,
            black spruce and muskeg behind them,
heading for the hard scrabble and old
            exhausted mining towns of Ontario.

Do you know where we're going?
            she asked. Finding himself in unfamiliar
territory, he didn't know how to
            answer. All he knew was they were
leaving Rupert's Land, the ancient
            kingdom of the fur trade, crossing
the Arctic Divide, the serpentine
            ridge that sunders the great waters in
two, driving into a foreboding solitude
            strewn with unanswered questions.

Lost Horizons

Once I gazed into her
          clear blue eyes
where I could see
          forever, I knew I'd
found the heart's
          haven, vowed I would
never be lost again.

Then Death crept in
          on quiet feet and
stole her from me.
          Now, though sunlight
holds her wherever
          I go, whenever I
try to reach her she
          slips away.

Yet, here I am, the
          sad dreamer, after
all these years still
          seeking the remembered
light I once found
          in her eyes—
the beacon to home.

Act of Communion

The souls of the dead
            speed faster than light,
sweep into the wide
            deep hands of God's
love. Sometimes when
            we close our eyes, isolated
and alone, lost in a
            dream of the twilight flickering
between birth and dying,
            their afterimages linger,
glow on our eyelids, and
            we hear the echo of their
soft voices.

Open wide your eyes,
            they say, *we are not far*
away and will
            accompany you. Have
faith, find us in
            the lush green divinity
of nature waiting
            for you, alive in the room
of your heart,
            now and forever.

Love Letter to My Wife
(for Kathy)

We've weathered some stormy skies, dear,
felt the hard, sharp elbows of the fleeting
years. Like twin trees, grown old rubbing
against each other, we've endured together.
Nothing shocks us much anymore, but who
would have believed we could hear the world
in a different key yet sing the same love song?

Look! The sun rises above the deckled
hills, lighting a broad blue sheet of waiting
sky and, already, waves of new tenderness are
washing upon the shore. Though age has
not been kind, we're still undaunted. Let's
be brave, go kayaking one more time.

Words We Neglect to Say

There's something I neglected to say
That came to me clear from the blue,
We need love, not bread, for our way.

Cold and brutish the day
When sun is hidden from view.
There's something I neglected to say.

Though marvelously fashioned from clay
We are chippy as chimps in a zoo.
We need love, not bread for our way.

Loyalties will often betray
And vanish like sparks in a flue.
There's something I neglected to say.

Malice can wrench us astray,
We are sheep who gambol on cue.
We need love, not bread, for our way.

Did I tell you this morning I love you,
And need you more than I knew?
These are words I neglected to say,
We need love, not bread, for our way.

THE ACHE OF ABSENCE

I find it difficult to let a friend or loved one
go into that country of no return.
I answer the heroic question
"Death, where is thy sting?"
with "It is here in my heart
and mind and memories."
—MAYA ANGELOU

The Ache of Absence

Always a departing
        train, a last wave and
the receding station,

dust devils and swirling
        roadside trash,
the face of someone

you love
        there one moment,
then gone…

waking in a house
        of viewless light,
unable to breathe.

Freeze-Frame of Memory

Last night I fell into
        a deep sleep, dreamt
I glimpsed your face as
        through a clear glass,
saw again the
        exacto knife beside your
bed, the thin gash on
        your wrist, the small crimson
trickle of blood,
        watched in mounting horror
as it morphed into
        a raging river sweeping away
all our dreams and hopes
        before it, only to
wake next morning
        to find the watermark of
your absence still there—
        an indelible dark stain
on my heart.

Lovebird of the Heart

As I lie in bed this morning,
> frazzled and discouraged after

another night of fitful dreams,
> the dogs of regret nipping at

my heels, I listen to the clapping
> of leaves as a dove strolls

across the sill of my bedroom
> window, a white feather in

its beak, reminding me of
> all the years I took so much

for granted…imagine you
> are there beside me again,

my beloved, and how just
> being with you would be

enough…grateful how swiftly
> the lovebird of the heart

can unlock our cell of memory,
> free us from the dark.

As the Spirit Whispers

Lost and desperate, I was away from
shore, floundering on the brink of waves tipping
me into danger, too far out to see. Adrift from
the world, the hills ceased to speak to me; an
impenetrable ceiling of darkness shadowed
my spirit. I began to see myself as a burden
to the happiness of loved ones, a house with no
windows. Tomorrow no longer belonged to me.

Don't bury my soul with my body, or allow one
blind act to define who I was or am. Let my
memory glow like fireflies in a jar behind your
eyelids. Together, my heart in yours, yours in mine,
let's believe that love and mercy, unbound by time,
can reach beyond this life and, like our gracious sun,
even melt endless fields of sorrow.

Sun Shadows

drift across the green hills
                on the far side of the lake—
dark slow-moving curtains opening
                roomfuls of light in their wake.
As I sit and watch, sunlight
                pauses to caress the cedar
tops surrounding me before
                letting go and moving on…

like us who hold dear ones
                in the soft warmth of our
arms, gentle pockets of sunlight who
                stay just long enough to leaven
our lives with light and love, but
                always moving on,
beginning and ending, waving
                goodbye again and again.

The Departed

never cease to
       haunt us—the loved ones
we didn't have a
       chance to say, or even wave,
goodbye to, who
       tore a gaping hole in
our hearts that never heals,
       spirits now, who become
the air we breathe—gather
       each evening at the
top of the stairs to cry out
       our names in soft, plaintive
voices, beckon us to join
       them. *Come with us,*
come with us, they sigh.

Two Tankas

There can be nothing
harsher and more dreadful on
this troubled planet
than being deeply in love
with someone Death steals away.

*

The black cloud that hid
the beautiful face of the
mountain drifts aside;
if only seeing you just
one more time were that simple.

A tanka is a 31 syllable classical Japanese poem

The Secret Passageway of Mercy

When grief comes unbidden and folds its
        dark wings round us, as surely it will,
you make a deep room for it inside
        where lost loved ones can dwell—a small
private place where no light of the day
        reaches and few see. But the dead don't
slip away quietly, refuse to let us forget,
        they cry in the night for a letter or kiss, claim
they've unfinished business to complete.

And sometimes, when weary and unable
        to sleep, we wish our departed would
leave us in peace, keep their desires and
        memories apart…but if that wish were to
come true how would we ever feel the
        healing power of tears, how deeply the roots
of love grow in the rich soil of the heart.

Midnight Epiphany

Sheet lightning outside,
     rain tapping lightly
on the steel roof;
     inside the cottage
snuggly in bed,
     drowsy, dreaming
of trivia and
     my beloved dead,

I'm suddenly aware
     of the infinity of
expanding stars
     above my head—
millions of bright
     shining eyes streaming
toward the ceiling
     of heaven as though
the thin veil between
     this world and the next
had torn open—
     think I hear
dim ghostly voices,
     shuffling of feet.

The Handyman

Last summer I watched as my handyman neighbour
at the cottage hauled out my old green fishing boat,
cut a swath of fibreglass matting, saturated it with
resin and patched it smoothly over the gaping hole in
the hull. *The boat will float again like new,* he
said proudly afterwards.

One year later I sit at his bedside in the hospital,
listen to his laboured breathing; he's closed his eyes,
neither moving nor speaking. An implacable tumour
is tunneling deep inside his brain and, unlike our
distempered goods that can be restored, nothing
anyone can do will fix it.

Change of Season

All her life a feeling of abandonment grieved her.
She could never justify in her mind why her mother
refused to hold or see her after her birth, and put
her up for adoption. At times she felt as though
she'd been cut adrift like a papier-mâché boat
to float into the future alone.

Nights when wet winds whipped the wild longings
of her heart, she'd try to draw her mother
close to her—imagining her doing dishes, hanging
clothes, or glimpsing her face on the glazed surfaces
of things. As she put to bed the babies of a different
life, did her mother ever regret her decision, she often
wondered.

The autumn morning, trees ablaze with colour,
she learned of her mother's death. She was suddenly
overwhelmed by a sense of gratitude for the miraculous
gift of breath and, for the first time in years, could
feel her mother's restless spirit hovering at her
elbow, waiting like her for a change of season—the
benediction of freshly falling snow.

Interrupted Dialogue

Sailing ships were his obsession, his way
to dialogue with pain. Days he'd spend
in his wheelchair, working on models,
trimming masts, rigging, planks with
delicate care. When the doctors urged him to
slow down, he'd tell them his life, like his
garden, was a never-ending work in progress.

Here his last schooner sits on his mantel: mast
uncut, sails, spars missing—unfinished like
a half-expired breath, its rush of urgent
syllables stayed. No movement now, even
his garden stilled.

Elegy for Eric

The sun that shone brightly that day,
        watched him leap from the high granite
cliff, fall like a fleeting shadow down
        the steep rockface, scrub oak and wild

junipers into the dark womb of the
        silent waiting lake. Neither bird nor beast
heard the quiet splash. Love ordered his
        youth—his mother's tenderness, his father's loyal
blessing. He'd grown tall, daring and lean.
        Now the guarded sweetness of his life
gathered to a close. Beautifully he

sleeps under the speechless moon in the
        forgetful blue kingdom. Not even
a father can wake him.

The Density of Regrets

I observe my old neighbour trudging home past my
house clutching his coat collar on this cold, blustery

January evening. I've only spoken to him once—a
casual encounter years ago when we first moved into

town. He stopped me, wanted to talk about his
brilliant, youngest daughter, a medical graduate,

and her death at twenty-eight from a brain tumour
but, at the time—still too stricken from the hammer

blow of my wife's suicide a few months earlier—I was
unable to respond to his sorrow. Later, I would often

wonder if it was our common bereavement that made
him want to talk to me. Now, twenty years later, my

failure to reach out and share his pain still preys
upon my conscience. Strangers we remain, wrapped

in the silence of our separate grief, passing under
white trees, almost invisible in the snowy night.

Another Kind of Waiting

The last time I visited my old friend at the hospital
          in the city where we grew up together, observed
the tubes protruding from his chest, the container
          on the floor beside the bed, half-full of fluid, dark
red, almost purplish—the colour of blood before oxygen
          reaches it—I confess I didn't know what to say or
do, so I rambled on about the past (such are the
          covert games we love to play) and he mentioned a
recent trip to Ellesmere Island, that treeless tundra in the
          Arctic where next to nothing grows.
Even polar bears avoid the place, he said, and
          how surprised he was that scientists had waited
so long to discover fossils deep within the ground,
          vestiges of a tropical rain forest that existed fifty
million years ago. Then he looked at me a
          long moment, answered my unspoken question:
The tests are done; there's nothing left to do, but wait.

You Are My Beloved
(for Bobby)

Buried deep in the unfathomable heart,
surrounded by darkness, the seed finds

a stony place. Patiently, we moisten its
tiny roots with life-giving water, make an

airy space for it to breathe and grow.
This can go on for a long time, till we

wonder if green shoots will ever come.
Then one morning we wake from troubled

sleep to find the hard earth broken and…
surprise!…an amaryllis blooming before

our awestruck eyes, a voice whispering,
I am Love and you are my beloved.

Reluctant Journey

Knowing he had no choice,
        he lifted the heavy stone into
his awkward arms,
        walked across the endless
fields, shifting its weight
        from time to time to ease
the pain, often stopping
        to lay it down and catch his
breath before taking it
        up again, befriending his
burden mile after mile till
        it became the weightless
ballast of his wounded life.

(inspired by Jack Gilbert)

The Lookout

They climbed the steep cliff of the hill to the
granite ledge at the top—their favourite lookout.
Free of the world's tug, they gazed at the distant
horizon and vast expanse of sky full of bright
promises, hugged, looked into the window
of each other's love-brimmed eyes where they
could see forever. *The hills of heaven wait,*
she said.

Little did they know, that sunny July afternoon,
that within a year she'd pierce the brittle
membrane between being here and being
elsewhere. Now all he could remember of the
day was the clear blue dome of sky, and how
light the green world felt in his arms.

Legacy of the Falls

Something must have beckoned
              her that Easter Sunday
long ago, a voice
              perhaps she couldn't name.
You need a break, she told
              him when they parted. Then
the police and the sudden cataract of
              details spilling like a ghastly
dream—how she parked and
              locked the car, blocked
the entrance to the police station, her
              keys and wallet poised neatly
side by side on the driver's seat,
              the camera she wore round
her neck the tourists saw when
              she mounted the parapet just
before she leapt, the peaceful
              look on her face as the powerful
rushing current swept her
              on her back over the brink.
O, the cool cunning of it all.
              And now this wound that never
heals—a never-ending waterfall.

No Balm for Open Wounds

As I was watering flowers in the
          garden of our dream home,
thinking of how they filled our life with
          joy and light, death slipped
in from behind a hedge when I wasn't
          looking, barred the door, robbed
us of everything we held most dear.

The children gather on our bed
          where we cling together
like survivors on a raft,
          barely breathing, our
knotted bodies a ring over
          the hollowed place
where she slept as though
          it still held her shape and
warmth, arming our hearts,
          our only defence against
the merciless dark.

The tipped bell makes
          no sound, the black sheet
of ice will not drift away and
          I'm helpless to tell them

anything that will ease their pain
        or explain why the
pathways of love are crossed with sorrow,
        that there is no balm
for the open wound of loss.

You're Never Ready

The sun was shining…or was it? Was this
the day you intended to dispense your
small cache of good deeds? Does it matter?

You see the police cruiser park across the
street from your home. Curiosity impels
you outside. Before you get a chance to brace
yourself, the news comes hurtling at you out
of thin air, slams into your face like an
Irishman's big-knuckled fist, and you see
yourself falling in slow motion, the hard
unforgiving pavement rising to meet you.

No Abiding City

No abiding city exists on this earth, not one;
Fate's only bad luck, not Providence dressed neat.
God doesn't pick favourites nor inflict pain for fun.

You take your beloved French poodle out for a run
only to witness her killed by a van on the street.
No abiding city exists on this earth, not one.

When evil riddles our world and we're stunned
we look for scapegoats to blame in others we meet.
But God has no favourites nor inflicts pain for fun,

and when someone we love dearly perishes young
grief gnaws at our hearts like salt in the deep.
Here on earth there's no abiding city, not one.

Adam blamed Eve for the Fall in the garden
but God drove both out into the rain and the sleet.
God picks no favourite nor plays demon for fun.

We, God's children, cry out to high heaven,
we're lost in His silence and scattered like sheep.
No abiding city's here on this earth, no, not one;
God doesn't pick favourites nor inflict pain for fun.

Survivors

Every day I wake in our same bed
        remembering you, see the light
growing outside the window,
        surprised another day's awaiting
me. As I go about my chores—
        the usual dull daily routines—
your shadow is never far away.

Come evening, I'll catch
        the late news on TV, or go out
to the odd movie where
        lovers never fail to evoke the
grief of your absence, then
        to sleep and dream again—small,
inconsequential threads that
        weave the fabric of the everyday,
my world the same, yet changed.

Before bed I'll go outside,
        keep vigil with the sky,
watch as stars wheel by,
        no longer asking why,

tell myself this poor pretence
        of going on is what the living do
with our brief leftover lives,
        just grateful to be alive,
each day the first day.

Poem for a Drowned Wife

You bred flowers, laughter, tears;
      love of family flamed in your heart.
You moved in circles of light with
      a kindness we will never forget.

Your path was a hub of forgiveness.
      When darkness fell like the weight
of escarpment and day was plunged
      into night—our waterfallen hearts

tossed into a cataract with no shores—the
      way of forgiveness you taught didn't
breed hate or make us orphans
      of light. O, lost one, now

on the fluvial bed where you lay…
      bones washed white as though by waves
of love…let the river that claimed you
      bless and keep you, we'll not dare

trouble or blame you; your body's home,
      no longer belongs to the air. You bred
flowers, laughter, tears; your kindness
      we will never forget.

Compline

Coppery light fluttering
        on cottage wall,

waves lapping
        on the shore;

summer and
        sunset and the

long arms of
        contemplation

reach out to me
        as I write this

poem, recall your
        face, long to hear

you whisper:
        All, all is well,

the sun—a crimson star
        dying in my eyes.

My Lovebird

was life and breath to me,
a gentle rush of wings. The

day she slipped off the husk
of gravity, climbed the long

blue staircase of sky and
disappeared, silence closed

me, cleaved my tongue. I
became a connoisseur of

absences. At night I'd shut
my eyes, cup my ears to the

starry heavens, *Lost
Lovebird,* I'd cry, *you must*

sing to me to be found,
but no sound rose to find

me, only a sigh from far away,
like the ebb of the sea, the

hush of a long goodbye.

When the Dead Are Still Near

In the wilderness of grieving—a trackless
wasteland of thorns and sinkholes—the
dead visit our solitude, whisper to us
from the other side of silence.

Take comfort from their companionship.
Wait patiently for what their voices, still
near, tell us.

The words of the dead strike sparks from
stones, light the path we all must go.

Winter Longing

Grief still clogs
> the branches of my heart;

each day that now passes
> I find it harder to draw comfort

from the stream of memory.
> But after a night of gently sifting

snow that laced the black limbs
> of my quiet wood with a

feeling of peace, the colour
> of my mind changed and I

thought I glimpsed the numinous
> afterglow of her presence—

a halo of light around her face—
> that made me yearn to reach

out and touch her pale white
> arms, forget for a moment

death's long, cold embrace.

Of Times Past

Tomorrow's another day and
      yet here I am again on

our cottage shore, gazing at the
      night's starred nakedness,

searching for your hiding
      place in the dark blue dome

of infinite space. But when I shout
      your name far and wide

across the sky, you never reply. O
      if only I could glimpse your

face and hear your voice once more
      before the new dawn breaks:

Look, look, a falling star.

On Becoming

Outside my window this New Year's
Day, a winter storm. Vital parts of my
soul, captured by the storm, are snowed
under, dispersed with old dreams in the
whitened wind.

Some days I feel like a man carted off
in the gathering dusk, pushed into a wide
cold river with no name—a destiny no
New Year's resolution can change.

There can be no turning back; let the
clocks run late. I have outlasted fear, now
trust my tired old body to take me each
snowy last step.

Grief

Grief's a heartless buccaneer
who wields a hidden, sadistic knife
to rip old scars that bleed red tears.

Lurking behind you very near
he'll ambush you in dead of night
for grief's a heartless buccaneer

who sees your peace as bounty dear,
his entitlement to steal—a right
to rip old scars that bleed red tears.

His master plan is based on fear
that shows no pity for your plight
for grief's a heartless buccaneer.

Your pain will never make him veer
once he's found his own delight
to rip old scars that bleed red tears.

Never in his long and stealthy career
has he missed a chance to strike
for grief's a heartless buccaneer
who rips old scars that bleed red tears.

THE MANY FACES
OF LIFE IN OUR WORLD

*Above all, walk with glittering eyes the
whole world around you, because
the greatest secrets are always hidden
in the most unlikely places.*
—RAOLD DAHL

Entrances and Exits

Coming into this world,

an orderly progression of

warmth and wonder await, but

leaving the world—a cold fate

no one escapes—the going

comes in no order at all.

Where Past and Future Meet

As I wander this deserted beach, haunted
by the ghosts of the sailors and colonists who
first landed here, I wonder if the beauty
of what-used-to-be dazzled their eyes as
they gazed in awe upon the pristine forests
that rolled back unendingly from the shore
and the long sunlit waves that broke with
promises of a green new world,

now: a desolate strand of ransacked dreams
strewn with plastic, broken glass, rotting
fish and oil-smeared seabirds...the defiled
sea tumbling in angry steel-cold waves.

Wake-up Call

Sometimes a whole civilization
        can be sick and dying and
we, like children, hijacked by
        the addictive "Now" in
our small, heated playrooms,
        go on pushing our myriad
"Consume Now" buttons,
        blowing bigger and bigger
coloured balloons until,
        in what seems like a blink-eye
of time, the ping of an
        incoming message pricks
our ears, tells us
        our coloured balloons are
about to burst, that
        it's time to change before
too late: surrender
        our short-term fixation
with more, bigger and better,
        and think Future.

Lament for a Sick Planet

Our planet is becoming a wasteland.

In the name of greed we've plundered our
oceans, turned them into dead zones of
plastic debris and toxins.

Our rivers and lakes stink of effluent.

We've exterminated entire species, clear-cut
rain forests and polluted the atmosphere.

Our bloated cities teem with the hungry
and destitute who ask where are the stars
that once whispered of hope?

How much longer can we march to the
furious drumbeat of profit?

The future looms before us like a loaded gun.

Retribution

We proceed at warp
        speed with our crimes
against Mother Earth.
        Rebels, ingenious fools
that we are,
        we spread our foul
contagion far and wide
        to air, sea and forest, even
polluting our hearts and minds.

But Earth, who
        neither forgets nor forgives,
bides her time, grows increasingly
        angry. Having drunk her
fill of insults for too long
        she's begun to lash back,
forces us to see her festering
        wounds, taste our toxic wastes.
We have sown
        a path of destruction,
will not escape her wrath.

El Salvador 2008

A fouled river in a spiny volcanic landscape
where hope is an impossible habit to break…

old women along the shore scrubbing shirts on
flat smooth rocks,
broad hands quick and rhythmic, icons
of the scarred history of their people
who smile, say little…

the faces of the young mothers of Ahuachapan
at the Centro Communitario
making plans for dry latrines and potable water
for their families, the future
mirrored in the shining eyes
of their children
entwined in their strong, brown arms—

hope at the end
of a long lightless tunnel
coming at the pace of oxen.

Cruising the Rideau

Travel the canal slowly, enjoy the scenery; your
voyage is not a race. The trip, not the finish line,

is the goal. Remember the canal belongs to everyone,
you're only a guest. Don't pollute it or treat other

voyagers with disrespect. Obey navigational signals,
they're there to keep you safe. Listen to the

lockmaster; only fools refuse direction. Locks are
sacred spaces, the up-and-down hinges of your trip.

Keep to the back of the chamber, avoid bumping
others; those who love turbulence court disaster.

Lastly, exit the locks peacefully in an orderly
single file, make no unnecessary waves, leave the

sound of gratitude in your wake.

What the Buddha Said

I came here to tell you certain things.
          Forget your fading map of cures, your

old life has not served you well. You
          are something the wind caught standing

fast asleep and then moved on.
          Learn to make peace with yourself

and others before it's too late.
          Do not defile the planet, it is your home.

Remember you are only passing
          through, a guest on Spaceship Earth.

The desert between kindnesses
          is cruel, be kind to everyone you meet,

even those who wish you ill.
          Loss comes to all, but beyond the frontier

of death the sun rises and
          the mountain keeps an echo deep inside

itself of every one you lost. Let
    the beauty you love be the beauty you do.

I will sit with you awhile; we
    will watch the stars wheel by. In the morning

I promise you will wake.

Broken Promises

We dream of an imagined
            perfection in the beautiful
edifice of our vast world—the
            buried gem in the tidal pool—
and yet, like pebbles skipping
            over the surface of the deep,
we never plumb the depths.

We excuse ourselves saying
            the time for transformation
is not ripe, our stars
            are not aligned. We're never
ready, always waiting for
            something more to happen, a
miracle perhaps, that will cure
            our guilt-ridden hearts.
Thus we muddle on in
            our cramped, messy way, as
though death were nowhere to
            be found, blind to the
homeless and destitute
            we pass on the street.

Only at the end, when we
         glimpse the mottled sleeve of time
in the mirror, do we ask
         what went wrong, hold the broken
fragments of our good intentions
         in our hands, weep for all the
promises we failed to keep.

The Happening

This poem is happening now, not yesterday,
or tomorrow, but this moment in the aches
and diminishments of aging.

This poem is not a grief-cry of human loss,
a lament for the lost honey of youth, nor just
a story on a bright string of words.

This poem is a mellowing, a happening and
lighting of lamps, the bringing forth of a new
kind of time. All manner of things—the daily

enactments of small acts of compassion and mercy,
our sun reaching down to hold us in its light and
warm our skin, the gleeful laughter of playground

children—beckon us to open our eyes and ears,
kneel before the gift of life. A new horizon is
opening to answer our prayer, bless and

be blest. This poem is happening now; a largeness
we can't explain is breaking in. Death is not
the only truth that lasts.

Progress

Warfare's a new game,
                        hand-to-hand combat's
obsolete. We've traded our pelts

for braided uniforms,
                        no longer wage war
with knives and clubs.

Hunched over our
                        powerful computers—
detached, safe, and far away—

we pinpoint our targets
                        with the cool competence
of judges with words,

dispatch drones to
                        do our dirty work…isolated
from the screams of victims,

our hands unbloodied,
                        consciences
clean and untroubled.

Zen Prayer

Enough of words! The mind has mountains
that block the Now's light.
No more divisions, outer and inner, high and low,
body and soul,
no more fancy locutions, false pieties,

only this inscrutable "isness"—
the I which is not I, the All in everyone,
the quiet music of cumulus clouds,
the hum of insects,
hummingbird's blurred wings and lapping water,
the fragrance of pines,
the bee lost in the sweetness of the blossom—

hidden notes of one seamless, harmonious whole
and the resonance of its sounding:
a soft voice in the silence whispering,
You are my beloved.

(*inspired by Thomas Merton*)

Exile

Homelessness is not just a word or
a name for any place you lay
your head,
a rain that soaks your bed, or
a freezing cold
that numbs your bones.

It means to be displaced,
to have your heart torn out;
it means to be uprooted from life
itself, to feel you don't belong.

It's a key you've lost,
a door you can't find,
a Christmas no longer yours.

The Song of Love

What does the song of love
mean to the lonely priest lost
in a dark wood, or

the desperate mother
with her withered dreams unable
to feed her children?

What does the song of love
mean to the abused child, the
unwelcomed, weeping refugee, or

the privileged One-Percenters in
their towers of greed parsing
Profit and Loss reports?

And the song of love…what does it
mean to despots with their grisly
calculus about who lives, who dies?

And you, divided America—land
of the free and home of the brave,
glitzy marching bands, and pennies

that trumpet your trust in God—
tell me, does the song of love
mean the same to you

as to the solitary nightingale
singing into the darkness for a new
dawn to break?

How I Envy

the chipmunk on the cottage deck this
     morning, cheeks bulging with peanuts
from my outstretched hand, who has
     no inkling of the rush and welter of
our anxious lives or the high rent
     we pay—suffering, loneliness, aging,
death—for the privilege of living
     in a changing and cruel world.

At dusk he races back to his hidden
     earthen home to rest for the night—
safe, snug and unaware of the galaxies
     spiraling above his head in interstellar
space, nothing to disturb his
     dreamless sleep.

The Gift

This lemon
    I'm offered,
old and shrivelled,
    only gives what
it is able, makes
    no pretence of
sweetness.

I accept the gift,
    pluck the fruit
from its husked
    roundness, taste
and eat one sour
    wedge at a time,

let its sourness
    purge my tongue,
humble all my
    old categories
of perfection.

Summer Storm

Dozing by the shore,
        swaddled in the sun's warm

embrace…out of the
        untroubled blue I hear a

distant rumble, then,
        in quick succession, see a dark

curtain hurtling
        toward me across the lake,

feel the first faint flutter
        of wind and droplets on my skin,

and, before I know it,
        a heavy downpour of brilliant

loud rain is pounding
        on my head, my cozy world upended…

the frantic race for cover.

Zen Poem

My head has grown white;

time to wave goodbye to all that,

snap the silvery chain.

No need to fear;

    beyond the dark gate

four sides, eight directions,

    unchanging light.

Coming, I clenched my fists;

going, I spread them wide.

One Day's Light

We come this way but once and yet, despite
our gifts, are heedless how our time is spent
against whatever's left of one day's light.

Old regrets, like steely mirrors, haunt our
nights with hurtful memories we still lament.
We come this way but once and yet, despite

angelic voices that strive to whet our appetite
to live, our straight intentions soon get bent
against whatever's left of one day's light.

To say there's scant relief for pain is trite,
but often true; grief's the currency of rent
we pay to come this way but once. Yet, despite

poems and prayers to make things right,
we puzzle long and hard where contentment
went against whatever's left of one day's light.

No matter our brave intent, we never quite
redeem the sullied moments and repent.
We come this way but once and, yet despite,
squander whatever's left of one day's light.

CONSOLED BY HUMOUR

Humour is everywhere in that there's
irony in just about anything
a human does.
—BILL NYE

Judge's Prayer

Take pity, Lord, on your earnest
          servants who twitch and wince

before deciding; forgive their
          flights of fancy that burst

like bubbles in a pot; grant them
          the solace of bringing law and

order to Your flock, and guide them
          over the slippery spots.

And when they make the beds we
          lie on, commit their little

gaffes and get overruled, I beg you,
          Lord, don't laugh.

"Afraid So!"

Did you say you charge
by the hour and you can't
guarantee I'll win?

If this gets in the
media will people think
I am money mad?

Did you say this is
not going to end well, that
I may lose the case?

Though he hates dogs, is
it possible he could get
my cockatoo too?

Did you mention that
this case has no end in sight,
could even be appealed?

If I lose on appeal
I might go bankrupt,
even lose my home?

You call this justice?
Shouldn't I've been told all this
before I started?

(inspired by Jeanne Marie Beaumont)

How to Cook a Judge

If you want to eat a judge you'll
have to stretch your imagination.
Unlike the python trying to eat an
elephant, you'll have to think small.

Begin by removing glasses, pens,
gold cufflinks, red sash—anything
that would catch in your throat and
spoil the meal. Clip off the ragged,

horny-nailed toes. Since judges dole
out their decisions in long, stringy
portions, you must slice them into
bite-sized morsels. There's nothing

more noxious than bits of old law
stuck inside the craw. Out of respect,
don't forget to leave a fig leaf; without
dignity, judges are inedible. And

baste your portions with scads of honey,
for judges taste best if swallowed sweet.

There Are Days

The giraffe plunders food from the tallest trees
        without having even the tiniest of qualms;
the proud lion who never finds fault with himself
        thinks nothing is wrong in killing his young.
The spider who deftly weaves webs of entrapment
        shows no remorse in the least in feasting on her
victims for lunch. As for the amphibian frog who
        hunts in the rain in a waterproof coat, guilt never

gets in under his skin. And even if the hippo looked
        into a mirror by chance, he'd never pause to wonder
if he's eating too much or aging too fast. Alas, all
        of these creatures live in the moment, unburdened
by the iron sled of guilt. I confess, Lord, there are days
        I wish You'd made us a little more like them.

The World I Love

Our whirling blue globe's often capricious
            and cruel, adds one trouble on top
of another without stop till your head
            starts to swirl and never, never
says she's sorry. Although sometimes
            angry and hurt, confused by what's
happening and tempted to leave,
            in the end I always forgive her—don't
ask me why—never want to part. Some
            call me a smitten old fool, but truth
is I'm still madly in love with that lovely
            old tart, and the thought that some
day we'll part is breaking my heart.

Parsons in Paradise
(for Tom)

With no flock to keep,
                nothing to do and
no sermons to rue,
                old parsons just
browse in heavenly
                pastures beyond
the world's reaching,
                savour the blessing
of a life without preaching,
                no longer lose
sleep over stray or
                lost sheep.

The Day of My Funeral

I take a seat in the back row at the
funeral home to catch the eulogies.
I'm wearing my good Oxfords and

a tasteful bow tie. Some I don't
recognize, but it's upsetting to see an
old acquaintance like Malcolm, who

never liked me much, saying things
now that I can't defend myself. And
who's that stranger with bedroom eyes

bending low to peck my wife on the
cheek? And listen to the Rev. Basil
Wadsworth, the bluff, brick-faced

clergyman, who's rattling on in a
God-rendered voice about himself,
me and God as though we were bosom

pals. Compassionate, wise, rescuer
of stray dogs—all that fulsome praise
makes my ears burn red. The words

don't fit, but its too late, there's nothing
I can do about this retrofit, but get up
and leave, go back home to bed.

(inspired by Willis Barnstone)

Obsession

Frustrated and restless, cloistered
indoors by the pandemic, the poet
reverted to words, his great obsession,
priming the pump of his imagination
in isolation—haiku after haiku pouring
forth in a cascade of motley images
that never seemed to end or satisfy.

When he began to forget to eat and sleep,
his wife told everyone she tried to help
but was forced to give up, learn the grim
lesson: you must never disturb a poet
when the divine frenzy's upon him.
He'll only stop when the well runs dry.

Coming Back to Earth

No matter how refined
                your wishes or
how distinguished you are,
                routine duties are never far.

Poets must climb down
                from ethereal spaces,
where their word games
                leave such dazzling traces,

to rinse and dry the
                rancid dishes; judges too
must leave their lofty places
                to clean their robes,

forget their status. No
                one's exempt, all must
wash their minds and faces
                in sudsy water.

The Anointing

When Chester, the pompous warrior
     of the legal arena, got the news of his
appointment to the bench something

astonishing and scary happened—he
     immediately began to levitate. At first
slowly, witnesses claimed, then at an

accelerating rate, he finally
     disappeared from view behind a thick
screen of white cloud. Thereafter

he was only seen on
     earth on rare occasions. Rumour
has it that if you are lucky enough

to be looking in the right direction
     at sunset, you might glimpse him
striding across the horizon in

his billowing silk robes of office,
     in the act of sharpening words for his
next important judgment.

Recently unverified sightings
    claim that bits of his splendid
rhetoric drifted down to earth

like stray confetti, somewhere in suburbia.

How to Forgive an Abusive Ex-Lover

I was impressed by his model behaviour
when he showed up at my doorstep the

other day disguised as a long-tailed
crustacean…the way he scuttled meekly

about my door, his blue-black carapace
shining in the sun, never once opening

his vicious shell-crusher claws. Though
I knew he wanted something, was up to

no good as usual, so moved was I by the
pitiable look in his sly stalk-like eyes that

I was briefly tempted to let bygones be
bygones and forgive him for the horrible

way he'd treated me. And later, after I'd
tossed him into the boiling iron pot, his

muffled wire-thin squeals almost made me
rue what I'd had to do. I must confess too

when I saw him all tricked out in his bright
red finery just before I ate him, I paid

him one last farewell compliment, told him
how elegant and handsome he looked.

A Headhunter's Report

Young but
mature.
Very bright.
Seasoned in intellectual combat.
Well-read.
Solid on principle.
Ambitious.
Not politically correct.
Not screen-obsessed.
Wants to leave his mark, make
the world a better place.

This candidate is none of these.
Should fit in well.

Limerick Lake Blues

On a day grey as stone, as the poet sat on his
dock feeling weary, worn and terribly alone,
a chipmunk dropped by, a glint in his eye, and

right off the bat started to chat. *I know your
big trouble,* he said in a nattery voice. *You
live in a bubble, but lest you pine to be dead*

*you've only one choice: you have to get out of
your skin to start living again, or go home
and do all your groaning and moaning in bed.*

That's when he darted away like a small gust
of wind, leaving the poet with nothing to say.
But he knew he was right: if your soul loses its

music it feeds on the static of old desires and,
knowing what was important had already been said,
he took the chipmunk's advice, went home to bed.

AS MY DAYS GROW LONGER

*Years may wrinkle the skin, but to
give up enthusiasm wrinkles the soul.*
—SAMUEL ULLMAN

Should Old Age

lay waste my intellect, wrap my
      senses in the grey cloak of night and
I no longer hear Your voice in the
      morning praise of songbirds, or see
Your fingerprint on the green lattice
      of spring—a stranger unto myself and

others—I pray, Lord, that You will
      not abandon me to unfathomable
dark, but draw me closer to Your
      breast as You would a beloved child,
breathe Your spirit into me to lift
      me up, help me break freely into new
fields of everlasting light where Your
      love never fails, goes on forever.

Old Age Lament

No longer can I hear the
   wild, plaintive calls of loons,
or the sweet voices of birds—
   their urgent, evening madrigals.

Even the gentle notes of wavelets
   lapping on the shore no longer
play for me. How I sometimes
   envy the staring owl, listening

in the dark, who hears it all.
   Certain parts of me are gone
forever and there's nothing
   I can do. Every dawn, it's said,

brings a fresh beginning, but
   late at night in bed I, who no
longer hear these songsters at
   their song, wonder how I will

ever get along. *A waste,*
   my wife laments, *not to hear*
the voice of nature in all her
   music. O, the sad partings of
old age! What poverty is mine.

The Years

creep up on me, steal the green
      from my world. Days merge
into grey, my "to-do" lists never
      get completed. *You're repeating*
yourself, dear, harps my wife.

At the county fair the tea reader
      said, Y*our wings are stuck to the*
cup. Today, as I gaze at water spiders
      zigzagging aimlessly on the dark
surface of the pond, I see my face
      reflected back. As my own life
skitters away, there's nothing left
      for me to do now except to pray.

In the Mall

the old-timers
      drift down the corridor—
rusty freighters
      looking for ports of call
that no longer exist—
      no destination but
the busy coffee
      shop at the end where
they love to
      anchor, sip coffee and
reminisce about
      the past, and where
the time went and,
      before they doze off
under the soft glow
      of distant skylights, ask
the unspoken question:
      What happens next?

The Traveller

A traveller arrives on a distant shore,
a faded map in his hand. He comes to
revisit old sights and sounds where he
once felt joy and everyone feasted on
the cusp of tomorrow—a time when
the invisible fire of love seemed
inextinguishable.

He soon discovers that the fabulous
dream he fastened together from old
memories has rushed out of sight into
the darkness behind him, changed into a
story with no sequel—only a few scattered
ashes in the kingdom of the moment.

On Looking at Obituary Photos

Caught in the freeze-frame of expectancy,
their youthful smiling faces betray no refusal

of the future that awaits them, and seem to be
trying to tell us something important: not

to fret, the end is not the gloomy ogre we dread
or imagine, but more akin to slipping down

a long smooth embankment with an old friend
into a wide welcoming river…or setting forth on

a long sea voyage for some mythic island of
perennial youth where the sun always shines

and our little stories spin on forever, leaving
no trace save this yellowing newsprint.

The Day of the Dead

Evening spreads its copper sheen
       across the October sky; birds retreat
to nest. An expectant feeling permeates
       the air. As the darkness thickens, the
moon edges into view and the first
       small signals of night wind herald

the coming transformation—
       erase the yawning gulf between the
living and the dead. In my dreams,
       all my lost loved ones will suddenly
reappear, rise and glow, radiant as
       I have never seen before, and I will
open my heart once more to the
       blessing of their beautiful presence.

Wintry Radiance

Snow floats down gently
        from the grey sky outside

my sunroom window this
        early morning, slowly

dissolving the darkness of night
        in waves of radiant light,

coating the black branches of
        my old crinkled apple tree—

with its gnawing memories of
        having lived too long on this

earth—under a soft layer
        of white forgetfulness.

The Slow Drawing Down of Shades

How did we get from there to here so fast?
we ask; everyone thought getting old would
take much longer. Now gradually, or suddenly,
we notice we're worn out, deflated by the
diminishments of living—a sudden fall,
cracked hips and ankles, memory gaps, all
the small cruel betrayals of body and mind...

until too late we learn that we've fallen away
from the world in dimming light, that there'll
be no more confident strides toward beckoning
horizons. And then in quick sequence, the high
stone wall, no reason to stay, the slow drawing
down of shades.

Vagaries of Time

The past:
     a relentless undertow
of half-forgotten
       memories.

The present:
     a race across winter
fields, slow
       erosions of the heart.

The future:
     an unending vista and
the sleep that fills it
       like drifting snow.

Missing Keys

In the seniors' residence
the widows, pale faces
    strafed with age,
sense the universe shutting down,
eat in silence in the dining room,
fidget with their forks, stare around
the room with forlorn blankness.

Afterwards—like the moon on a winter's
night edging through rifts of clouds—
they cautiously push their walkers down
long, unending corridors, tired eyes
full of questions, wondering
    where they put the house key
to their lost homes.

In the Nursing Home (a suite)

A widow sits in her wheelchair in the garden, birds silent, a small dog for company. She's trapped in a long, dark tunnel, her inner map astray—nothing in her closet of old memories to help her find an exit.

*

Clinks of cutlery on plates, frail voices of bent slack figures plodding back to their rooms, the lonely whisper of closing doors. In the dining room, a single straggler pauses to peer wistfully out the window at the darkening welt of sky.

*

There is little in the way of good news here, grey walls await death. Everything seems provisional, an unfinished rehearsal. A bald man steers his wheelchair into a crowded corridor, waves a broken wristwatch and mutters, *Goddamit, can't anyone fix anything around here?* An ageless crone with yellow hair, legs splotched green and black, winks, whistles and wails. A woman, strapped into her chair, a sock doll in her arms, tosses me a girl's smile and announces, *You're a good man, I can tell.* Taken aback I ask, *How do you know that? Everybody's good here,* she says, her voice shining like a splinter of hope in the dark.

The elderly, minds gutted by the pitiless fires of aging, shuffle into the movie room, but even an old favourite—*Singing in the Rain*—and an exuberant Gene Kelly can't keep them awake. They nod off, in search of youthful dreams locked inside the cedar chest of memory.

*

She lives alone on the third floor of the residence, has not had a visitor for years. When anyone asks her age she tells them: *I don't remember how old I am.* Like a vagrant cloud she appears and drifts along the corridors, opening and closing doors, inquiring if anyone has seen her missing children. At night she is startled awake by the voices of her children in the hallway outside her door. On Mother's Day she greets the staff and shows an orderly a bouquet of scrawny red carnations in her small white fist. *Look,* she says, *a gift from my children.*

Salt of the Earth

For years, in the cold-knuckled dark
of winter days, she'd rise in the small
morning hours while her ailing husband
was still asleep, stack the grate in the
kitchen stove, rake the ash pan to trap
the dying embers, polish his shoes,
prepare lunch pails and breakfast till
stars winked out and the white fan of
dawn appeared.

In the nursing home, a widow now, bent
and crippled with pain, she still goes about
trying to lighten the load of others with a
kindly word and cheery smile, inquires after
their health and children and, if they're
feeling low, patiently listens to their long
litanies of woe.

Who is this woman? you ask. She's part of
an invisible company of people whose small,
unsung labours of love leaven the world, stop
it from falling into darkness. Her name is
Hope; we call her Salt of the Earth.

Who Will Come?

Who will come to catch me
     when I stumble and fall, spirit
battered, nerves unhinged?

Who will come and sit to hold
     my heart, soothe my wounds
till fresh endurance grows?

And who will wait unwaveringly,
     for healing's touch and I
am strengthened and restored?

A friend.

WITH HEARTFELT THANKS

*Acknowledging the good that you already
have in your life is the foundation
for all abundance.*
—ECKHART TOLLE

Yes

to the lazy buzz of living,

yes to curlicues of moonlight in a garden,

yes to swimming naked, letting go,

yes to many bloopers and misdirections,

yes to my notebook, the missing pages, the words unsaid,

yes to dreams collapsing and happy endings,

yes to the unravelling yet forgiving heart,

yes to touching fingertips, the warm silk flesh of love,

yes, for someone near to bless,

yes to life and …
     yes and yes.

The Six Freedoms of Old Age

Freedom from the fear of aging.

Freedom from the need to hide our wounds
and appear invulnerable.

Freedom to enter into solidarity with
everyone we meet—our brothers and
sisters on the same human journey.

Freedom to be open to others' griefs,
listen to their experience and gently
touch their pain.

Freedom to empower others to share
their own freedoms of aging.

Freedom to bequeath an enduring legacy
of creative aging and gratitude for life
to our families.

Frail Fellowship

My old neighbour sat in his rocker by the
window, wrapped in a frayed housecoat,
staring at a distant wood, the room freighted
with painful memories.

The quality of his life was now measured
in visits to the doctor; the green tongues
of trees no longer spoke to him. I placed
the plate of food on his table. *I'm lonely,*
stay awhile with me, he pleaded. *I need*
someone to tell me why I'm still alive.
But I had a busy schedule, told him I had
to leave, promised to come back later.

Now it's too late. Last night he crossed the
threshold of the great darkness we all must
enter. How often we allow our flimsy excuses
to make us forget, Lord, we are all part
of the frail fellowship of the wounded.
Have mercy on our derelictions.

Prescription for a Good Life

Break free from your cell
        of darkness on the quiet

breath of prayer, open
        your eyes, eager to venture

into morning light
        with its great white

sheet of sky overhead
        to write on. Inhale

the pristine air,
        grateful to be alive.

At every green moment
        along the way, share

your hopeful spirit far
        and wide, trusting that

even if sunlight dims the
        earth will bloom again.

Let your hands overflow
          with good deeds like the

river of night shimmering
          with stars.

Morning Light

Some questions for you, reader:

Do you still bump into those
places where you say "No"
when you ought to say "Yes"

or your feet still pull you blindly
down dark streets trying
to find yourself?

Like me, you have trouble with
tenderness, can't find a clear
light, refuse to open your eyes
and ears, right?

Then this haiku's for both of us,
friend:

Bells of light ring in
the trees; *I'm here, here,* the sun
says. *Time to wake up.*

Blessings

Not being welcomed into this world is our
greatest wounding. A son seeks his father's
blessing to know he's cherished, a daughter
the grace of her mother's unconditional love
to know she's beautiful. The rejected
refugee, the homeless, the infirm and aged
often feel invisible, need to know they belong.

A blessing is akin to a lily opening on
dark waters, or the sweet trace of trust in
a small child's voice. Hidden blessings fill
the clean mould of the everyday, make small
temples of the fleeting moments—a nurse,
at the bedside of an elderly Covid patient,
smiling encouragements…the words *I love
you* from the lips of someone you care for…
or just a stranger who opens a door for you
to pass first.

We are blessed when we stand astonished
before the universe with its trillion stars
spinning through the night, knowing we have
the gift of life, are beloved of the earth.

There Are Times, Lord

I wake with the rising sun,
           peace brimming my heart—
no need for the distorted
           logic of memory, or a new moon,
to bring good news and
           lift me out of my self-defeating
ways.

I lay back and contemplate
           Your light streaming through
my window, content to listen,
           patient as a stone, to early
birds gossiping among
           themselves, the silver music
of birches in the breeze—
           small reminders of Your
myriad blessings, of all I
           can never be dispossessed.

Prayer of Thanksgiving

Knowing we are only earthen vessels passing through,
and that soon or late the pitiless waters will close over

us—wash away every vivid moment that graced our lives
and made us human and unique—let us be grateful

for all unearned miracles that come our way: the
glittering shores of distant galaxies, the way a cobweb

strung with dew sparkles in morning light, the joyful applause
of birches in the breeze, the opening eyes of the person

we love next to us at daybreak, all the many blessings
great or small, which we too often take for granted,

that make us feel beloved of the earth. Help us believe,
Lord, that beyond our mortal unremembering nothing is

ever lost in Your sight, that all our memories are enfolded deep
within Your merciful heart forever.

Litany in Praise of Water

Praise to you, Water…
           of the rolling tides,
quencher of dry wells.

Praise to you, Water…
           of the healing springs and
bountiful seas.

Praise to you, Water…
           of the stream of light,
dew of morning grass.

Praise to you,Water…
           chalice of thanksgiving
womb of creation.

Praise to you, Water…
           handmaid of the altar
and miracle of wine.

Praise to you, Water…
           river of rebirth
and breath of the Spirit.

Praise to you, Water…
                    Wisdom's bright jewel,
vessel of the eternal Word.

Silver Linings

There are always silver linings to raise
our spirits above our grey, ravaged
earth. Even when the weather turns cruel,
the light hard and shiny—like the sharp blade
of this January morning—and everyone
locked in bleak winter thoughts shivering in
their bones, small rays of sunlight still
break through.

Look! This morning sky, a translucent sheet
of azure blue, and children on the sidewalk, heads
tilted upward, mouths rounded in silent awe
at eaves—the icicles splintering and crackling
like glassy suns falling in their eyes.

Survivor

Observe the dandelion. Put aside your
conventional mind. Study her habitat:
hanging pots, lawns, meadows, sidewalk
cracks and vacant lots.

See how she lusts for light in all kinds of
weather, defies the grey death of asphalt
by thrusting her yellow head through
layers of paved convenience, the hardened
earth. Note how the bees of summer sip
her wine. Let her wanton beauty twinge
the heart, startle your inner dullness.

The dandelion is not an impediment to
progress; in the midst of adversity, she
teaches us how to live.

Spring Canticle

Out of the depths of this harsh winterscape,
Lord, You've answered my prayer. The

first faint blush of green kisses the trees,
bird calls bounce off the pale blue ceiling

of sky, apple blossoms float in the fresh
clean air like clouds of winged snowflakes.

Spring dances back in her pink lace finery,
seedlings of hope pinned to her sleeve,

scatters the stiff-necked winds and numbing
cold with a wave of her gentle hand.

Stanza by stanza, earth gives birth to a
new poem. Who could have imagined

Mercy's breath and largesse? On such days
you wish you could stay forever. There are

many ways to kneel and bless the earth.

Spring Prayer

How harrowing the world sometimes appears
in its heart-rending mystery. Before the blank
face of death, everything we love seems fragile
and fleeting—who will remember us when we're
gone, we ask? Yet we still wake from winter's
long white sleep yearning to shed last year's
impediments, our hearts aflame with the hope
of undying things, the whole earth our home.

Come, O Creator of the budding trees, the vine
that nourishes our branches with the sap of life,
let your leaf-light kindle the earth with the green
fires of Your love, free our restless hearts
from the bondage of dead dreams, raise us to new life.

Spring Longing

Winter retreats—remnants
            of soiled snow still cling to the
ground. Age silts the stream of
            memory; my mind is cluttered,
laced with old promises
            of fresh beginnings. I long
to mingle my breath again
            with the breath of blossoms,
restore my frazzled soul,
            but there's nothing I can say
or do but surrender to the
            grace of the moment, wait
for the prodigal sun to open
            its fist like a sheltering palm,
gently wake the buds from their
            long, green dream.

Hidden Lake

Leave the frenzied city where you slog it out each day,
discontent sizzling in your blood.

Find the hidden lake of dreams waiting for you all
these years.

When you arrive, let the silence seep into your soul. You'll
know you've come to a new beginning.

Go down to the welcoming shore, breathe in the cool moist
air. As your heartbeat slows and the weight of worry drops
from your brow, utter your own unspoken prayer.

Gaze at the white river of stars flowing across the roof
of night, hear the sucking sound of gloom disappear
through a million blue pinholes.

Feel the clasp of joy fasten the frayed edges of your life.

Shed your city clothes, dive naked into the healing water,
trusting it will hold you up.

Stroke by stroke swim out into grace.

Morning Surprise

Another fitful night. Outside,
        sirens blare, an ambulance
speeds past followed by a car
        full of prayer. Grief skids by
faster than love and I'm
        powerless to stop it. Then, just
when I'm beginning to feel despondent—surprise:

the moon, a pearly bobble in
        the sky outside my window,
clinging to the blouse of morning,
        a solitary robin caroling
cheerie, cheer up to the
        bright candle of the sun.

A Moment of Grace

Does anyone know what grace is? It comes
and goes like a tremor of light. Around the

campfire last evening, our faces glowed with
love and friendship, and the ordinary shed its

earthiness as we breathed in the majesty of
your creation, Lord, whose centre and ambit

are everywhere. A solitary heron rowed
across the purple scrim of low humped hills,

fireflies lit their tiny lanterns in the darkened
air, and the first perfect star edged out from

behind a bank of cloud. Under cover of dusk,
the energy of earthly light poured heavenward

as frogs began their chant of praise to the dying
sun, as if death were only a hollow husk

and their chant would never end. How beautiful
Your dwelling place, O Lord.

The Virtues of Solitude
(a meditation)

Solitude and social distancing can bring
blessings.

Solitude takes us out of our busyness, liberates
us from our fixation with material needs and
social distractions.

Solitude lets us see the world "as it is", draws
us inward to find our consolations and peace,
makes us realize how greatly dependent we
are for our happiness on nature, community
and the love of family and friends, how deeply
their absence wounds us.

Solitude makes room for the cultivation of
the soul, gives us the opportunity to focus our
attention on important questions. What is
central to being human? Does technology
control us or do we control technology?
Is making a living the same thing as living?
Is improving a house better than improving
our soul? It helps us avoid coming to the
end of our days and discovering we haven't
lived.

Solitude teaches us that anything that does not bring us fully alive is too small for us, puts us in touch with our creative and spiritual powers, opens our eyes to the poetry and mystery of life.

Solitude whets our thirst for Goodness, Beauty and Truth.

Thanksgiving Prayer

Thank You, Lord,
           author of the book of life,
Creator of the invisible
           neutrino and Milky Way,
black holes, roses
           and dandelions, rolling
clouds overhead,
           soft moss underfoot, the
sun and fully ripened grain.

Thank You, Lord,
           for the gift of rain and
the small green-braided
           garter snake, strawberries
hidden in a tangle of
           broad green leaves, the
ponderous elephant, plants
           and species of every hue,
shape and size.

But thank You most, Lord,
           for the gift of a loving and
grateful heart, You
           who are the True Vine and
sustainer of body and soul,
           fountain of living waters,
our pledge and our hope
           of eternal life. Amen.

Becoming a Senior

Now that I'm losing my hair and nearing
            the edge, hear death pecking at my ribs,
certain facts are becoming clear.

I'll never ski to the South Pole,
hang-glide off a glacier,
or become the world's fastest yodeller...

never win the Nobel prize for chemistry,
star in a Hollywood blockbuster
or be a sumo wrestler,

Grand Chess Master, astronaut,
world champion spear thrower...
            I can forget, along with
astrophysics and the Internet. I'll readily
admit certain things will never fit.

But that's okay, I don't intend
            to grumble or to sulk;
death's an insult on all our plates
and I'd be an ingrate to complain...
after all, I'm still alive, loved
and been loved, and while

the mystic rose of contentment eludes
　　　　　　me still
I can proclaim: I love my breath,
my sparrow light in this glade of dark,
nothing to sneeze at
　　　　　　eighty-eight.

True Freedom

Like birds who were
        created for flying,
your first and destined
        sky is deep within
you. Before the sun's
        transit is complete,
dare to open wide
        your wings and fly.

Have no fear of
        heights, you were
born to reach
        the stars, catch
the falling
        broken things.

(after Li-Young Lee)

EPILOGUE

New Year's Dream

In the dream I saw the woman at the gate of the
year, a blue garland in her raven hair, holding
aloft a lantern. *I have passed through a dark
valley,* I cried, *known thorn and thistle, felt the
cold claw of death in the tall reeds and now,
fearful and alone, I've lost my way. Why, woman,
have you brought me along this bitter path?*

But the woman at the gate of the year, beautiful
and serene only smiled. *Traveller,* she said,
*do not fear. The road to tomorrow lies off in the
darkness beyond your mortal eyes. I will give you
this lantern, whose windows—gentleness, hope,
trust and compassion—guard the flame of love to
guide your feet. Through the windings of your
journey hold it high. If you walk within the circle
of its light, it will lead you to the city on the hill
where all dreams end and tears are turned to
laughter.*

So sweetly did she whisper in my heart, so gently
did she smooth my brow, the sting of death was
soon forgotten and slowly, slowly, the beloved
child in me was born again to joy.

INDEX OF POEMS

BIOGRAPHY

James Clarke was born in Peterborough, Ontario. He attended McGill University and Osgoode Hall, then practiced law in Cobourg, Ontario. In 1983, he was appointed to the Bench and served as a judge of the Superior Court of Ontario. He is now retired and resides with his second wife, Kathy, in Guelph, Ontario.

Clarke is the award-winning author of twelve collections of poetry – eight of which have been published by Exile Editions – as well as three memoirs: *The Kid from Simcoe Street* (Exile Editions 2012); *A Mourner's Kaddish: Suicide and the Rediscovery of Hope* (Novalis 2006); *and L'Arche Journal, a Family's Experience in Jean Vanier's Community* (Griffin House, 1973). In addition, the *Legal Studies Forum* of the University of West Virginia College of Law has published nine collections of James Clarke's law poems. His work has been widely anthologized both in Canada and the United States.